Touchstones 4

OAKHAM SCHOOL

Name of Scholar to whom issued	House	Form	Date of Issue
Amanda Bowbow	B	6	JRW
ST ~~YEUCH IXIGERY~~			
Fred Smith	T	4	30/2/'83
Smith Cooke	C	3	?
Penny Lancaster	T	4^3	12.11.82
Somebody SEXY			
Gordon Man		Condom machine	
Danger Pick		A condom	

This book is the property of the School, and must be looked after carefully. It must be kept covered, and must not be written in.

NEW SCHOOL SERIES

Consulting Editor: R. Stone, M.A., M.Inst.P.,
Second Master, Manchester Grammar School

General Editor (Arts): B. A. Phythian, M.A., B.Litt.,
Headmaster, Langley Park School for Boys, Beckenham

Starting-Points
G. P. Fox, M.A.
B. A. Phythian, M.A., B.Litt.

Listen
An Anthology of Dramatic Monologues
W. A. Thompson, M.A.

Storylines
An Anthology of Short Stories
W. A. Thompson, M.A.

Considering Poetry
An Approach to Criticism
Edited by B. A. Phythian, M.A., B.Litt.

Poetry Workshop
M. G. Benton, M.A.
P. Benton, M.A.

Touchstones 4

A TEACHING ANTHOLOGY

MICHAEL BENTON M.A.
Lecturer, School of Education,
University of Southampton

PETER BENTON M.A.
Lecturer, Department of Education,
University of Oxford

HODDER AND STOUGHTON
LONDON SYDNEY AUCKLAND TORONTO

Contents

iv

PART B

SATIRES AND OPINIONS

WAR

Poetry for Supper P38

To the Teacher

The idea of 'teaching poetry' – certainly if the phrase is used in any formal, pedagogic sense – is, in itself, suspect: why, therefore, have we compiled a 'teaching anthology'? Briefly, we felt that there was a need for an anthology which offered more than a collection of poems. Poetry lessons depend so much for their success upon a sympathetic relationship between teacher and pupils and, although books will not in themselves create this relationship, they can help considerably by suggesting ideas for discussion, by showing different approaches to poems, and by encouraging pupils to write poetry themselves. We have attempted to satisfy these needs while avoiding the danger of setting out too rigid a procedure. We hope, too, that the teaching material we include will provide some useful starting-points for teachers looking for fresh ideas.

The pattern of our 'teaching anthology' is as follows. First, in Part A, we introduce three main topics which give information about a particular aspect of poetry, illustrate by examples, point questions and provoke discussions. The individual teacher is the best judge of just how and when to use this area of the book. We anticipate, however, that he might find material for about a dozen lessons in Part A and we have indicated by asterisks where possible sub-divisions of the material might be made. To attempt to structure lessons further than this, we felt, would be too inhibiting to the teacher. Secondly, in Part B, we have grouped the material so that the teacher will be able to deal with several poems, linked by some common quality of technique, subject matter, style or attitude, in any one lesson or sequence of lessons. Thirdly, at the end of most sections in Part B, we have provided a number of suggestions for encouraging the pupils to write their own poems, in the belief that it is just as important to get a child to write poetry as it is to encourage him to appreciate and criticise. We consider that it is vital that pupils should be allowed the chance to write, to experiment, to play with words and sounds, even with the shapes of poems in the same way that they are allowed free expression with paints and plastic materials in an art lesson. Through this kind of personal involvement comes an understanding and appreciation of what they read and, above all, an understanding of themselves and the world around them.

Although we do suggest certain lines of thought, we do not wish the books to be followed slavishly as a 'course'. Indeed, the distinction between material suited, for example, to a third as opposed to a fourth form must sometimes be arbitrary. Although we have numbered our books one to five and have chosen our topics and poems to suit particular age-groups, the teacher will find sufficient flexibility in the arrangement to be able to select and modify the material we print according to his own tastes and the abilities of his pupils.

Creative Writing

There are many ways of stimulating children's writing and every teacher has his own methods. We feel it would be presumptuous to give too much direction and we have, in the main, limited ourselves to suggestions in the creative writing sections. However, we do feel that rather different emphases are needed in the middle-school years: the moodiness and unpredictability which indicate the emotional changes going on in many children of fourteen or fifteen are familiar to all teachers of fourth-year pupils. In the creative writing sections, therefore, as in the anthology, we have aimed at providing material which in several ways will help children to cope with their own growing-up. First, we have made use of their increasing awareness of themselves by inviting them to write poems which require them to sort out their own feelings and attitudes towards experience. Secondly, we have suggested topics for discussion and writing which give children the chance either to show a wider social awareness or to come to terms with more complicated ideas and feelings: the sections on school and war, for instance, should help here. Thirdly, while we would still encourage pupils to write free verse, it is our experience that middle-school children often like the discipline of writing in regular patterns. Using the forms of some of the poems that we anthologise as models for their own verse affords *some* children the satisfaction of having a recognisable pattern of words at which to aim. The manipulation of rhymes, syllables, and metres can help them to define the boundaries of their poems and gives direction to their ideas without sacrificing the original spontaneity and feeling. For others, however, anything more structured than a seventeen syllable haiku proves inhibiting; but, whatever the reaction of the individual pupil to writing in a particular form, there is no doubt that some appreciation of the difficulties of writing in regular patterns is gained and this, in turn, helps the pupil to enjoy poetry more fully as well as become more discriminating in his reading.

The suggested approaches to creative writing are all ones which we have found successful. If teachers wish to pursue the subject of children's writing further, we would recommend the following books: Ted Hughes, *Poetry in the Making*, chapters one to five (Faber); Robert Druce, *The Eye of Innocence* (Brockhampton Press); Brian Powell, *English Through Poetry Writing* (Heinemann); and M. Langdon, *Let the Children Write: An Explanation of Intensive Writing* (Longman). We have found pictures and photographs invaluable as 'starters', particularly in that they focus attention on detail and help children to *see* as well as to look. We hope that teachers will also use other stimuli – e.g. music, or objects brought in by pupils and teacher – when appropriate. Large and colourful reproductions of paintings can be useful; abstracts as much as more representational works often fire the imagination. Paintings by Kandinsky and Miró have been found particularly successful. There are also many good photographs available in magazines and colour supplements which are easily mounted and may be used as starting-points for original writing. A file of these will grow rapidly.

The introduction of unusual and interesting objects may help to develop awareness and sharpen the senses – making writing more detailed, more exact, and, above all, more spontaneous. It is likely that most teachers already use this method, but it may be of interest to note some of the objects that we have found to arouse a strong response: driftwood, oddly shaped branches, twigs, roots and tubers are all particularly effective both visually and in stimulating a desire to *touch*. Textures are often strongly felt and pebbles, shells, conkers and bones may also be used primarily for the tactile response, though there is obviously much else besides.

With the co-operation of the Biology department, skulls, bones, skeletons and living creatures may be borrowed and studied in detail. Leaves, feathers and pine-cones are other natural objects which have fascinating structures and are easily obtainable. Lighted sparklers have also proved a successful device. All senses are brought into play here – one can even taste the faintly acrid smoke – and a real firework, however tame, evokes many memories of bonfire night. Soap bubbles, as produced by those canisters of bubble mixture into which a wire ring is dipped, are beautiful to look at, move in an unpredictable fashion and vanish in a most satisfying way. There is no reason, of course, why all these stimuli – particularly the visual material – should not be used as a basis for prose writing as well as for poems.

A final word: poems cannot be written on demand and we would emphasise that in using the Creative Writing sections teachers should encourage discussion of our suggestions and not present them to the class as 'exercises' which must be completed. Our own open-ended questions in these sections are not meant in any way to dictate the nature of the pupil's response: they provide stimuli which the pupil should feel free to ignore if he so chooses, or to adapt in the light of his own experience.

M. G. B.

P. B.

PART A

IMAGES

If you imagine something you make a mental picture of it – a mental *image*, and when the word 'image' is used it may be helpful to remember that, basically, it means nothing more complicated than 'picture'. A poet works largely through images and tries to create pictures in our minds through the skilful use of words.

We all use images in our everyday speech – usually without being aware that this is what they are. We try to create vivid pictures in the minds of our listeners: 'He slammed the ball home like a rocket'; 'He was as miserable as sin'; 'Hurry up, you snail!' An image presents a clear picture and, like a painting, is more quickly understood than words. Images are a kind of shorthand. You can easily see this by looking at some of the animal images that are used to describe people – we have already used 'snail'. Someone may perhaps be described as a slug or a snake-in-the-grass, a toad or a louse – you can probably add many other examples of the same sort. A whole range of unpleasant ideas is conjured up by calling somebody a slug. Try to list some of these. What would it mean if somebody was described as a lion? a rabbit? a rat? an old trout?

In the following poem the writer describes men admiring a girl in an open-air tea-garden in Egypt. He sees them as different kinds of fish.

Behaviour of Fish in an Egyptian Tea-Garden

As a white stone draws down the fish
she on the seafloor of the afternoon
draws down men's glances and their cruel wish
for love. Her red lip on the spoon

slips in a morsel of ice-cream. Her hands
white as a shell, are submarine
fronds sinking with spread fingers, lean
along the table, carmined at the ends. *painted red.*

A cotton magnate, an important fish
with great eyepouches and golden mouth
through the frail reefs of furniture swims out
and idling, suspended, stays to watch.

A crustacean old man, clamped to his chair
sits near her and might coldly see
her charms through fissures where the eyes should be;
or else his teeth are parted in a stare.

Captain on leave, a lean dark mackerel
lies in the offing, turns himself and looks
through currents of sound. The flat-eyed flatfish
sucks on a straw, staring from its repose, laxly.

And gallants in shoals swim up and lag
circling and passing near the white attraction;
sometimes pausing, opening a conversation:
fish pause so to nibble or tug.

But now the ice-cream is finished, is
paid for. The fish swim off on business
and she sits alone at the table, a white stone
useless except to a collector, a rich man.

KEITH DOUGLAS

How does his use of fish images help you to see each of the different characters?

Why is the girl described as a white stone? What does this perhaps hint at in her character?

*

It is primarily through pictures – images – that the poet gives us new ways of looking at things, new 'insights' into the world. The word poet means 'maker' and it is true to say that he makes or creates new insights largely through his use of comparison. When a poet describes bats 'like bits of umbrella' we see why he makes the comparison and can see the dark, stretched membrane of skin between the fragile bones. Neither bats, nor umbrellas, will be quite the same again! This is the poet *making* a new image from putting together two quite ordinary things. In this way a great deal may be said in a very short space. Samuel Becket in his play *Waiting for Godot* writes

> They give birth astride of a grave, the light
> gleams an instant, then it's night once more.

It is a terrifyingly stark image of human life and compresses so much into so few words.

In this poem by Ted Hughes there is a remarkable compression of ideas through the use of images.

Sugar Loaf

> The trickle cutting from the hill-crown
> Whorls to a pure pool here, with a whisp trout like a spirit.
> The water is wild as alcohol –
> Distilling from the fibres of the blue wind.
> Reeds, nude and tufted, shiver as they wade.
>
> I see the whole huge hill in the small pool's stomach.
>
> This will be serious for the hill.
> It suspects nothing.
> Crammed with darkness, the dull, trusting giant
> Leans, as over a crystal, over the water
> Where his future is forming.

4

What is the 'hill-crown'?

What effect is given by using the word 'whorls'?

Why is the water 'wild as alcohol'?

What previous hint or suggestion is the poet picking up when he uses the word 'distilling'?

Why a 'blue wind'?

What effect is given by the word 'whisps'?

What mental picture do you get from the fifth line 'Reeds, nude and tufted, shiver as they wade'?

There are two ways of interpreting the sixth line. What are they?

What picture do you form of the hill from the description in line nine?

What kind of 'crystal' has the poet in mind and what meaning does this give to the last line?

Why do you think he gives the poem the title 'Sugar Loaf'?

If you were to write down all the ideas that came to mind as a result of reading this poem carefully you would certainly fill many more than the eleven short lines it takes up. Again, it is the compression of ideas expressed through images which is responsible.

*

A somewhat different use of imagery can be seen in this poem by George Herbert, a seventeenth-century writer who was a parish priest:

The Church-Floore

> Mark you the floore? that square and speckled stone,
>   Which looks so firm and strong,
>   Is *Patience*:
>
> And th'other black and grave, wherewith each one
>   Is checker'd all along,
>   *Humilitie*:
>
> The gentle rising, which on either hand
>   Leads to the Quire above,
>   Is *Confidence*:

But the sweet cement, which in one sure band
    Ties the whole frame, is *Love*
        And *Charitie*.

Hither sometimes Sinne steals, and stains
    The marble's neat and curious veins:
But all is cleansed when the marble weeps.
    Sometimes Death, puffing at the doore,
    Blows all the dust about the floore:
But while he thinks to spoil the room, he sweeps.
    Blest be the *Architect*, whose art
    Could build so strong in a weak heart.

You will see at once that the stones of the church floor stand for some of the different Christian virtues and that the poem is really a kind of parable where everything symbolises something. Can you think of any biblical parables that work in this way?

Here is another poem by the same writer. Again, each abstract idea is made concrete and easily understandable by the use of images. After you have read the poem discuss some of these images and ask yourself why Herbert chose them.

The Pilgrimage

I travell'd on, seeing the hill, where lay
    My expectation.
A long it was and weary way.
The gloomy cave of Desperation
I Left on th'one, and on the other side
    The rock of Pride.

And so I came to Fancies meadow strow'd
    With many a flower:
Fain would I here have made abode,
But I was quicken'd by my houre.
So to Cares cops I came, and there got through
    With much ado.

That led me to the wilde of Passion, which
            Some call the wold;
      A wasted place, but sometimes rich.
Here I was robb'd of all my gold,
Save one good Angell, which a friend had ti'd
            Close to my side.

At length I got unto the gladsome hill,
            Where lay my hope,
      Where lay my heart; and climbing still,
When I had gain'd the brow and top,
A lake of brackish waters on the ground
            Was all I found.

With that abash'd and struck with many a sting
            Of swarming fears,
      I fell, and cry'd, Alas my King!
Can both the way and the end be tears?
Yet taking heart I rose, and then perceiv'd
            I was deceiv'd:

My hill was further: so I flung away,
            Yet heard a crie
      Just as I went, *None goes that way*
And lives: If that be all, said I,
After so foul a journey death is fair,
            And but a chair.

It is a parable or *allegory*. If you have read Bunyan's *Pilgrim's
Progress* you will know what that means.

Some things can be made real and immediate only through the use
of images. Abstract ideas are often communicated in this way. Here
is a poem by Philip Larkin that puts quite a complicated idea into
easily understood images.

Next, Please

Always too eager for the future, we
Pick up bad habits of expectancy.
Something is always approaching; every day
Till then we say,

Watching from a bluff the tiny, clear,
Sparkling armada of promises draw near.
How slow they are! And how much time they waste,
Refusing to make haste!

Yet still they leave us holding wretched stalks
Of disappointment, for, though nothing balks
Each big approach, leaning with brasswork prinked,
Each rope distinct,

Flagged, and the figurehead with golden tits
Arching our way, it never anchors; it's
No sooner present than it turns to past.
Right to the last

We think each one will heave to and unload
All good into our lives, all we are owed
For waiting so devoutly and so long.
But we are wrong:

Only one ship is seeking us, a black-
Sailed unfamiliar, towing at her back
A huge and birdless silence. In her wake
No waters breed or break.

PHILIP LARKIN

It *is* difficult to grasp the abstract. It might be worth discussing
your own ideas about, for example, God, heaven, hell, time, death.
How do you visualise them? Perhaps you could write a poem around
your own mental images of these; one possible starting point might
be to look at the picture on p. 9. Its title is 'The Healer'. – Why
do you think the painter called it this? How do you react to what
you see? What images are being used and why? Perhaps you will
find ideas for a piece of your own writing here.

8

Healer, *Magritte*

The poet is often faced with the task of expressing the inexpressible. We have all experienced love, hate, fear and a vast range of contradictory emotions, yet it is a real challenge to get these feelings on to paper in such a way as to make the reader feel exactly what we felt. In this situation, particularly with modern poetry, images are often strongly personal and whilst they obviously mean something to the writer they may not immediately have a precise meaning for the reader. You will probably be aware of pop songs where groups of images are used to create a mood or feeling, but where a *precise* meaning is difficult to find — even unnecessary.

We are not suggesting that the poem which follows has no meaning — it has — but it is perhaps more a meaning that is *felt* through the strange nightmare image of the crabs rather than a meaning which is spelled out clearly. When you have read the poem, discuss what you saw in your mind's eye as the images developed.

Ghost Crabs

At nightfall, as the sea darkens,
A depth darkness thickens, mustering from the gulfs and the
    submarine badlands,
To the sea's edge. To begin with
It looks like rocks uncovering, mangling their pallor.
Gradually the labouring of the tide
Falls back from its productions,
Its power slips back from glistening nacelles,[1]
    and they are crabs.
Giant crabs, under flat skulls, staring inland
Like a packed trench of helmets.
Ghosts, they are ghost-crabs.
They emerge
An invisible disgorging of the sea's cold
Over the man who strolls along the sands.
They spill inland, into the smoking purple
Of our woods and towns — a bristling surge
Of tall and staggering spectres
Gliding like shocks through water.
Our walls, our bodies, are no problem to them.

[1] outer casing of an aeroplane's engine

Their hungers are homing elsewhere.
We cannot see them or turn our minds from them.
Their bubbling mouths, their eyes
In a slow mineral fury
Press through our nothingness where we sprawl on our beds,
Or sit in our rooms. Our dreams are ruffled maybe.
Or we jerk awake to the world of our possessions
With a gasp, in a sweat burst, brains jamming blind
Into the bulb-light. Sometimes, for minutes, a sliding
Staring
Thickness of silence
Presses between us. These crabs own this world.
All night, around us or through us,
They stalk each other, they fasten on to each other,
They mount each other, they tear each other to pieces,
They utterly exhaust each other.
They are the powers of this world.
We are their bacteria,
Dying their lives and living their deaths.
At dawn, they sidle back under the sea's edge.
They are the turmoil of history, the convulsion
In the roots of blood, in the cycles of concurrence.
To them, our cluttered countries are empty battleground.
All day they recuperate under the sea.
Their singing is like a thin sea-wind flexing in the rocks of a
    headland,
Where only crabs listen.

They are God's only toys.

TED HUGHES

Salvador Dali's picture 'Landscape: the Persistence of Memory'
which you will find on pp. 12 and 13 has a similarly haunting and
dream-like quality. Again the images seem to stand for something –
but what? Discuss with the other members of the class just what you
see and what you think it means. You could try to write a poem of
your own either using this picture as a starting point or taking a
related subject such as 'Time'.

Landscape: the Persistence of Memory, *Salvador Dali*

FORMS

RHYME AND METRE

In order to understand the particular forms we shall discuss later in this section, we need to look briefly at two of the devices which writers sometimes use to give their poems shape and unity.

Nursery rhymes are usually the first contact we have with rhymed verse: there is a certain satisfaction, even in these simple jingles, in hearing the words form themselves into a regular pattern. Perhaps you can recollect some of those which you enjoyed as children and, if you do not consider yourselves above such things, you could usefully spend some time examining these and seeing just how simple their rhymes and rhythms are. If you have a younger brother or sister at the nursery rhyme stage you will usually find that he or she takes great pleasure in supplying the rhyming words at the ends of lines if you omit them when repeating the verse. The predictability of the rhyming sounds contributes a good deal towards this pleasure, and, through their regular repetition, rhymes act as a sort of 'cement' which helps to bind a poem together. If rhyme is used well, that is, if it appears to flow naturally into the poem without any distortion of word order or meaning, then it has the effect of making the poem express its meaning clearly and succinctly. Notice how the rhymes contribute to the witty expression of this poem.

The Grey Squirrel

Like a small grey
coffee-pot
sits the squirrel.
He is not

all he should be,
kills by dozens
trees, and eats
his red-brown cousins.

The keeper on the
other hand,
who shot him, is
a Christian, and

loves his enemies.
Which shows
the squirrel was not
one of those.

HUMBERT WOLFE

In discussing the ideas and expression of this poem you may want to
comment on the effect of the rhymes. Would the poem be better with-
out them?

In addition, rhyme can give a sharp edge to a poem – sometimes a
cutting edge which the poet deliberately uses to wound his subject,
as Pope does in his portrait of Lord Hervey (p. 112). Many of the
most bitingly critical words in this passage are also the rhyme
words – 'stings', 'annoys', 'bite', 'betray', 'squeaks', 'toad', 'lies',
'blasphemies', 'antithesis'. Similarly, rhymes are often used in short,
cleverly worded poems which have a pointed meaning: these are
called epigrams. Here is an example:

I am his Highness' dog at Kew;
Pray tell me, sir, whose dog are you?

ALEXANDER POPE

15

Shadows, Rome. *Photo: Michelangelo Durazzo*

Using this poem as a model, perhaps you could write an epigram of your own.

All poets constantly experiment, in one way or another, with the seemingly endless possibilities of their raw material – words. Experimentation of a very obvious kind – parodying another poet's style or trying out different verse forms – often comes early in a writer's life. Here is an example from the work of Wilfred Owen. Before the outbreak of the war, Owen was living in Bordeaux and, as a young writer, he experimented with word-sounds, particularly with rhyme and half-rhyme. The poem which follows is an interesting one in that it shows us half-rhymes at the beginning of the lines and full rhymes at the end. The collection of simple word-pictures which it comprises may remind you of a series of Japanese haiku poems:

16

From My Diary, July 1914

Leaves
    Murmuring by myriads in the shimmering trees.
Lives
    Wakening with wonder in the Pyrenees.
Birds
    Cheerily chirping in the early day.
Bards
    Singing of summer, scything thro' the hay.

Bees
    Shaking the heavy dews from bloom and frond.
Boys
    Bursting the surface of the ebony pond.

Flashes
Of swimmers carving thro' the sparkling cold.
Fleshes
Gleaming with wetness to the morning gold.
A mead
Bordered about with warbling water brooks.
A maid
Laughing the love-laugh with me; proud of looks.
The heat
Throbbing between the upland and the peak.
Her heart
Quivering with passion to my pressed cheek.
Braiding
Of floating flames across the mountain brow.
Brooding
Of stillness; and a sighing of the bough.
Stirs
Of leaflets in the gloom; soft petal-showers;
Stars
Expanding with the starr'd nocturnal flowers.

WILFRED OWEN

What is the difference between half-rhyme and full rhyme? A good
way to appreciate sound effects in this poem is to imitate the style.
Try to write a poem in the same pattern: pairs of lines which use the
same devices as Owen uses – half-rhymes and full rhymes. Choose
your own subject: it is probably best to attempt a series of loosely
linked word-pictures on a fairly broad subject – a season of the year,
night, weather, cities, reflections, shadows – and to record clearly
and simply the impressions in your mind's eye. If you choose the last
suggestion the picture on pp. 16 and 17 may help you. Its oddity has
been increased by printing it in a rather unusual way.

*

You will be familiar with the idea that poems have rhythms: a poet
uses different rhymes to express different feelings. These long, slow-
moving lines at the beginning of one of Shakespeare's sonnets sug-
gest, by their rhythm, a thoughtful, unhurried state of mind:

When to the sessions of sweet silent thought
I summon up remembrance of things past. . . .

Contrast these lines with the mood of Ariel's song, which expresses
the delight of this spirit of the air as he is about to regain his freedom:

Where the bee sucks, there suck I
In a cowslip's bell I lie;
There I couch when owls do cry.
On the bat's back I do fly
After summer merrily:
Merrily, merrily shall I live now
Under the blossom that hangs on the bough.
(from *The Tempest*, Act V, sc. 1)
WILLIAM SHAKESPEARE

How would you describe the rhythm of this song? How does it help
to convey Ariel's feelings?

The rhythm of a poem, then, is not chosen accidentally: it fits in
with the poet's mood and his feelings towards the subject he is writing
about. Nor is a poem's rhythm organised accidentally, for, under-
lying the rhythm of many poems, there is a mechanical pattern which
is called metre. There are a number of different metres in English
poetry and their rather forbidding names describe the number and
position of the stressed and unstressed syllables within the line of
poetry. Iambic metre is the simplest and commonest. An iambus is
one light syllable followed by one heavy one. Most frequently it
appears as a series of five iambuses, making up the most popular
metrical pattern in English poetry, the iambic pentameter. Here is an
example from Shakespeare:

Nŏ lóng/ĕr moúrn / fŏr mé / whĕn Í / ăm deád
Thăn yoú / shăll heár / thĕ súr/lȳ súll/ĕn béll. . . .

This metrical rhythm is quite easy to imitate: it is like repeating the
word 'again' five times. Try to write a few lines of your own in this
metre. Choose any subject which interests you, but aim at technical
accuracy.

19

It is unnecessary here to go into detail about other commonly used metres. What is important is to realise that by using a metre a writer gives his poem a rhythmical pattern which helps him to capture in words the feeling of what he is writing about. This is not to suggest that a lot of poems are written in regular metres throughout. Few poems are, for poets are aware that repeated regular rhythms become boring. You will find, therefore, on reading through the anthology in Part B, that there are a great many variations worked on basic metrical patterns – variations which reflect changes in feeling, pace or attitude which occur as a poem develops. In 'pop-song' terms, metre usually acts as a sort of 'backing' against which the poet composes a variety of melodies.

FREE VERSE

Many poems, especially those of pre-twentieth-century writers, have metre, but there are many others which have no metre at all yet are still rhythmical.

Animals

I think I could turn and live with animals, they are so placid and
    self-contain'd,
I stand and look at them long and long.

They do not sweat and whine about their condition,
They do not lie awake in the dark and weep for their sins,
They do not make me sick discussing their duty to God,
Not one is dissatisfied, not one is demented with the mania of
    owning things,
Not one kneels to another, nor to his kind that lived thousands of
    years ago,
Not one is respectable or unhappy over the whole earth.

WALT WHITMAN

Here is a poem with neither metre nor rhyme, yet it does have an irregular rhythm. How would you describe its rhythm?

Poetry which is written in this way is called 'free verse'. Modern poets, in particular, have used this form frequently and you will find

20

many examples in Part B. The words of a free-verse poem are not organised into a symmetrical pattern and yet it would be wrong to think of this form as being 'formless'. In good free verse the shape and structure of the poem reflect the mood and meaning of the writer: the organisation of the lines and verses arises directly out of what the poet wants to say. One of the best writers of free verse is D. H. Lawrence. You may well have come across some of his animal poems before – *Bat, Mosquito, Mountain Lion* or *Snake*: here is the opening of another animal poem, *Baby Tortoise*:

You know what it is to be born alone,
Baby tortoise!

The first day to heave your feet little by little from the shell,
Not yet awake,
And remain lapsed on earth,
Not quite alive.

A tiny, fragile, half-animate bean.
To open your tiny beak-mouth, that looks as if it would never
    open,
Like some iron door;
To lift the upper hawk-beak from the lower base
And reach your skinny little neck
And take your first bite at some dim bit of herbage,
Alone, small insect,
Tiny bright-eye,
Slow one,
To take your first solitary bite
And move on your slow, solitary hunt.
Your bright, dark little eye,
Your eye of a dark disturbed night,
Under its slow lid, tiny baby tortoise,
So indomitable.

When discussing this picture of the tortoise – the details Lawrence selects, the comparisons he uses, the character of the animal he creates – ask yourself also about the form of the passage. What decides the length of the lines? Why do we have two short sections followed by a longer one?

You may well have written some free-verse poems of your own already but, now that you have had the opportunity to discuss this

21

form more fully, try it again. Choose your own subject — there is no need to write about animals unless you wish to — but remember to exploit the main advantage of this form, that is, the freedom that you have to concentrate exactly on what is in your mind's eye without the distractions of rhyme or metre. One temptation that you must resist is that of simply writing what is really a prose composition chopped up into varied line lengths. Make sure that you leave out any words which are not earning their keep and be sure that there is always a reason for lines being the length they are. Work over your first version with these ideas in mind until you feel it says what you want it to say in the most economical way possible.

*

RHYMING COUPLETS

Of all the forms that employ rhyme and metre the simplest is the couplet of two similarly constructed lines, bound together by rhyme. Here are two examples: the first simply expresses the writer's enjoyment of waking early in the morning.

> To hear the lark begin his flight,
> And, singing, startle the dull night,
> From his watch-tower in the skies,
> Till the dappled dawn doth rise;
> Then to come, in spite of sorrow,
> And at my window bid good morrow,
> Through the sweet-briar or the vine,
> Or the twisted eglantine. . . .
>
> (from L'Allegro)
JOHN MILTON

The second extract is in quite a different mood — a satirical attack upon someone the poet disliked:

> Damn with faint praise, assent with civil leer,
> And, without sneering, teach the rest to sneer;
> Willing to wound, and yet afraid to strike,
> Just hint a fault, and hesitate dislike;
> Alike reserved to blame, or to commend,
> A timorous foe, and a suspicious friend. . . .
>
> (from Prologue to the Satires)
ALEXANDER POPE

22

As you can see from this passage, one advantage of the rhyming couplet when used for satiric purposes is that the last word of the first line remains echoing in the mind long enough for its counterpart in the second half of the couplet to enforce the attack by its sound as well as its sense.

You should find it fairly easy to master the couplet form, but, as with all rhyming patterns, the danger is to allow the rhymes to dominate your meaning to such an extent that your poem becomes artificial or awkward. With practice you will find that the couplets come more naturally into your head and your poems will improve. Take care, then, that you do not produce more rhyme than reason. On this occasion use the above extracts as models for your own verse: you may want to write about some experience which has made you feel very happy, as in the first passage, or perhaps you could attempt a short satire in the style of Pope's poem.

*

BALLAD

If the couplet is the simplest form, the ballad is the most natural of metrical forms for English to adopt. You will all know something about the early ballads – poems which set out to tell a story, one which was not simply read but sung. Singing and story-telling are two of the most popular and enjoyable pastimes in any society and the singers of medieval England chose the ballad form for their narratives of fighting and love, their tales of mystery and the supernatural as instinctively as, in more recent times, writers have used the ballad in work songs and 'pop' lyrics. Because this form is so common and because of its oral, rather than written, origins, there are not only several versions of many ballad stories but there are also many variations of the basically simple ballad form. The basic form is illustrated in the following poem:

The Wife of Usher's Well

There lived a wife at Usher's Well,
   And a wealthy wife was she;
She had three stout and stalwart sons,
   And sent them o'er the sea.

23

They hadna been a week from her,
  A week but barely ane,
When word came to the carlin[1] wife,   [1]old
  That her three sons were gane.

They hadna been a week from her,
  A week but barely three,
When word came to the carlin wife,
  That her sons she'd never see.

'I wish the wind may never cease,
  Nor fashes[2] in the flood,   [2]troubles
Till my three sons come hame to me,
  In earthly flesh and blood!'

It fell about the Martinmas,
  When nights are lang and mirk,
The carlin wife's three sons came hame,
  And their hats were o' the birk.[3]   [3]birch

It neither grew in dyke nor ditch,
  Nor yet in ony sheugh[4];   [4]trench
But at the gates o' Paradise,
  That birk grew fair eneugh.

'Blow up the fire, my maidens,
  Bring water from the well!
For a' my house shall feast this night,
  Since my three sons are well.'

And she has made to them a bed,
  She's made it large and wide;
And she's ta'en her mantle her about,
  Sat down at the bedside.

Up then crew the red red cock,
  And up and crew the gray;
The eldest to the youngest said,
  ''Tis time we were away.'

24

The cock he hadna craw'd but once,
      And clapp'd his wings at a',
When the youngest to the eldest said,
      'Brother, we must awa.

'The cock doth craw, the day doth daw,
      The channerin[5] worm doth chide;   [5] fretting
Gin we be mist out o' our place,
      A sair pain we maun bide.

'Fare ye weel, my mother dear!
      Fareweel to barn and byre!
And fare ye weel, the bonny lass,
      That kindles my mother's fire.'

                                        ANON

What has happened in the story?

A good story-teller sketches in the background to his tale quickly
and concentrates on moments of suspense and interest. Does the
ballad-writer achieve this balance here?

Discuss the form of this poem: what is the rhyme scheme and the
metrical pattern of each verse?

Does this form seem apt for story-telling?

Why not try to write a ballad of your own? Ballads, as we know,
lend themselves to action, adventure or mystery: when you have
chosen your story – it may be a historical incident which appeals to
you, a cowboy tale or a love story, or something of topical interest –
decide carefully on your metre and rhyme. Once you have these clear
in your mind you will find that your ballad develops surprisingly
quickly. There may be someone in your class who can play a guitar:
if so, one or two of the ballads could be given musical accompani-
ment or you may be able to bring to school records of modern or
folk ballads.

*

SONNET

The last form which we want to introduce to you will make more
demands on your ingenuity than any of the others. The sonnet is at
once one of the most intricate and most satisfying forms to master,
and, if we deal with it step by step, you should be able to understand

the pattern of a sonnet even if you have some difficulties to sort out when you come to writing one of your own.

The first thing to realise is that this form gives the writer a precise framework for his ideas as it must be composed of fourteen lines, each one an iambic pentameter (look back to p. 19 to remind yourself of the metre). These two rules govern all sonnets, but the rhyme schemes vary according to which of the two types of sonnet the poet is writing. The Italian (or Petrarchan) sonnet consists of eight lines, called the octave, rhymed on two sounds, and arranged as two four-line units, *abba abba*. In the remaining six lines, called the sestet, two or three new rhymes appear, often arranged as two three-line units, *ccd ccd* or *cde cde*, or, as in this example, *cdc dcd*.

> The world is too much with us; late and soon,
> Getting and spending, we lay waste our powers:
> Little we see in Nature that is ours;
> We have given our hearts away, a sordid boon!
> This sea that bares her bosom to the moon;
> The winds that will be howling at all hours,
> And are up-gathered now like sleeping flowers;
> For this, for everything, we are out of tune;
> It moves us not. – Great God! I'd rather be
> A Pagan suckled in a creed outworn;
> So might I, standing on this pleasant lea,
> Have glimpses that would make me less forlorn;
> Have sight of Proteus rising from the sea;
> Or hear old Triton blow his wreathèd horn.
>
> WILLIAM WORDSWORTH

The English (or Shakespearean) type of sonnet, however, is constructed in three four-line units and a couplet. The rhyme scheme, therefore, is usually *abab, cdcd, efef, gg*. Sometimes there is a shift in the thought of the poem between the octave and the sestet – as commonly happens in the Italian sonnet – but often the poet will smooth over this division and, instead, use the final couplet as a unifying and summarising point of the poem. Here is an example:

26

Sonnet 73

That time of year thou mayst in me behold
When yellow leaves, or none, or few, do hang
Upon those boughs which shake against the cold,
Bare ruin'd choirs, where late the sweet birds sang.
In me thou see'st the twilight of such day
As after sunset fadeth in the west;
Which by and by black night doth take away,
Death's second self, that seals up all in rest.
In me thou see'st the glowing of such fire,
That on the ashes of his youth doth lie,
As the death-bed whereon it must expire,
Consumed with that which it was nourish'd by.
  This thou perceivest, which makes thy love more strong,
  To love that well which thou must leave ere long.

WILLIAM SHAKESPEARE

When you are discussing these two sonnets pay particular attention to the form of both poems: make sure that you can follow through the pattern in each case, for, if you understand their construction, your own sonnet-writing will develop much more readily.

In order to help you see how a sonnet can emerge from a sequence of disorganised and often badly expressed ideas we have printed, on the following pages, the first and last of Wilfred Owen's four drafts of his famous war poem, *Anthem for Doomed Youth*. They will help you to appreciate the careful and painstaking work that has gone into this piece, and demonstrate the huge contrast between the writer's hesitant jottings and his final, tightly written poem. You may be able to deduce some of the reasons why Owen exchanges one word, line or image for another. Here are a few points to take up:

How formed is the sonnet in draft 1?

Is this a regular English or Italian sonnet, or are there variations?

Do you agree with Owen's final decision about the title? Why might he prefer 'doomed' to 'dead'?

Compare the opening four lines in the two versions and try to account for some of the changes.

Does Owen make alterations simply to change the meaning of his words, or for other reasons as well? For sound-effects? rhythm? feeling?

27

Anthem for Dead Youth.

What passing-bells for these who die so fast?
 — Only the solemn [monstrous] anger of our guns.
Let the majestic insults of their mouths
 Be as the priest words [requiem] of their burials.
Of choristers and holy music, none;
 Nor any voice of mourning, save the wail
The long-drawn wail of high far-sailing shells.

What candles may we hold for these lost souls?
 — Not in the hands of boys, but in their eyes
Shall shine the many candle flames:
Our Women's wide-spreaded arms shall be their wreaths
And pallor of girls' cheeks shall be their pall
Their flowers, the tenderness of mortal minds
And each slow Dusk, a drawing-down of blinds

First Brought [Draft]
('With Sassoons amendments.)

What passing-bells for these who die as cattle?
    — Only the monstrous anger of the guns.
    Only the stuttering rifles' rapid rattle
Can patter out their hasty orisons.
No {~~music for all them~~, ~~nor~~/mockeries for them; ~~from~~} prayers ~~or~~ nor bells,
    Nor any voice of mourning save the choirs,
The shrill demented/~~disconsolate~~ choirs of wailing shells;
And bugles calling ~~sad across the~~ for them from sad shires.

What candles may be held to speed them all?
    Not in the hands of boys, but in their eyes
Shall shine the holy glimmers of goodbyes.
~~And~~ The pallor of girls' brows shall be their pall;
Their flowers the tenderness of {silent patient ~~——————~~} minds,
And each slow dusk a drawing-down of blinds.

[Pencil words were written by
S.S. when W. showed him the
sonnet at Craiglockhart in
Sept. 1917.]

Fourth and final draft

Once you have spent some time talking about Owen's poem, we suggest you attempt this form yourself. Choose your own subject, and, as before, try to reconcile what you want to say with the demands of rhyme and metre.

MAKING A POEM

In the previous two sections we have discussed images and forms –
images giving a mental picture of ideas or feelings, forms giving them
shape and definition. In this section we want you to read and talk
about some poems in which the writers explore their job as artists
and where, inevitably, they show us images and forms working
together to make their poems.

The Thought-Fox

I imagine this midnight moment's forest:
Something else is alive
Besides the clock's loneliness
And this blank page where my fingers move.

Through the window I see no star:
Something more near
Though deeper within darkness
Is entering the loneliness:

Cold, delicately as the dark snow,
A fox's nose touches twig, leaf;
Two eyes serve a movement, that now
And again now, and now, and now

Sets neat prints into the snow
Between trees, and warily a lame
Shadow lags by stump and in hollow
Of a body that is bold to come

31

Across clearings, an eye,
A widening deepening greenness,
Brilliantly, concentratedly,
Coming about its own business

Till, with a sudden sharp hot stink of fox
It enters the dark hole of the head.
The window is starless still; the clock ticks,
The page is printed.

TED HUGHES

A poem about making a poem.

Why does Ted Hughes use the title *The Thought-Fox* instead of simply *The Fox*?

At several points you are perhaps aware of the poem's appeal to your senses. Which of your five senses are involved as you read the poem and where?

Which do you find the more vivid and real, the actual world of the poet's study or the imagined world of the fox emerging from the forest?

Does the use of a four-line verse control the poet's thoughts *strictly*?

What effect, if any, does the mixture of rhymes and half-rhymes have in the poem?

Perhaps you have noticed how the poem returns to its point of departure in the writer's study. At the beginning the poet is sitting at his table, doodling on a piece of paper, gazing into the blackness of the night through the window. This blackness seems itself to be an image of his own mental blankness until the fox enters his mind's eye. Notice how the 'starless window' reasserts itself in the last verse after the fox vanishes.

You may be able to put yourself in a similar situation by clearing your mind of its immediate interests and focusing your attention on some featureless object which can allow pictures to form in your imagination – a window, a sheet of paper in front of you, a wall. When an image forms itself, try to write down words, phrases, sense-impressions to capture this image as clearly as possible. From these notes you can, perhaps, make a poem.

*

Here is another poet, seated by a window, preparing to write.

Digging

Between my finger and my thumb
The squat pen rests; snug as a gun.

Under my window, a clean rasping sound
When the spade sinks into gravelly ground:
My father, digging. I look down

Till his straining rump among the flowerbeds
Bends low, comes up twenty years away
Stooping in rhythm through potato drills
Where he was digging.

The coarse boot nestled on the lug, the shaft
Against the inside knee was levered firmly.
He rooted out tall tops, buried the bright edge deep
To scatter new potatoes that we picked
Loving their cool hardness in our hands.

By God, the old man could handle a spade.
Just like his old man.

My grandfather cut more turf in a day
Than any other man on Toner's bog.
Once I carried him milk in a bottle
Corked sloppily with paper. He straightened up
To drink it, then fell to right away

Nicking and slicing neatly, heaving sods
Over his shoulder, going down and down
For the good turf. Digging.

The cold smell of potato mould, the squelch and slap
Of soggy peat, the curt cuts of an edge
Through living roots awaken in my head.
But I've no spade to follow men like them.

33

Between my finger and my thumb
The squat pen rests
I'll dig with it.

SEAMUS HEANEY

The writer's situation is similar to that of Ted Hughes in the previous poem, but the development of the thought is different. The poet's attention is taken away from his writing by hearing his father digging beneath his window. As he watches his father at work there form gradually mental pictures of his father digging potatoes and his grandfather cutting turf twenty years ago, when the poet was only a small boy.

What does the writer admire about the work of his father and grandfather?

What feelings does he have about his own work as a poet in the last three lines?

Are your senses involved as you read this poem too? If so, where?

Clearly, this poem does not have such a regular form as the previous one. What decides the shape of the verses?

This poem is built around a memory – a strong visual recollection from the writer's childhood. All of us can remember people, incidents, moments of happiness, sadness or fear from our early years. If there is a particular memory of this sort which you recall vividly, you may be able to write about it as Seamus Heaney has done.

*

In the first poem of this section Ted Hughes is concerned with showing us how a poem is written: in the poem by Seamus Heaney, the poet affirms a belief in the value of his work. How does Brian Patten regard poetry and the poet's role in society in the following piece?

Note to the Hurrying Man

All day I sit here doing nothing but
watching how at daybreak
birds fly out and return no fatter
when it's over. Yet hurrying about this room
you would have me do something similar;
would have me make myself a place
in that sad traffic you call a world.
    Don't hurry me into it; offer
no excuses, no apologies.
Until their brains snap open
I have no love for those who rush
about its mad business;
put their children on a starting line and push
into Christ knows what madness.

    You will not listen.
'Work at life!' you scream,
and working I see you rush everywhere,
so fast most times you ignore
two quarters of your half a world.
    If all slow things are useless
and take no active part in nor justify your ignorance
that's fine; but why bother screaming after me?
Afraid perhaps to come to where I've stopped
in case you find
into some slow and glowing countryside
    yourself escaping.
Screams measure and keep up the distance between us:
    Be quieter –
I really do need to escape;
take the route you might take
if ever this hurrying is over.

BRIAN PATTEN

Do you find yourself in sympathy with Patten's criticisms of modern
life?
    What do you think he regards as being most valuable for him as a
poet?

*

The poems which follow have been included here because, in different ways, they all show us the poet assessing his work as a writer. Read through these pages and compare the poets' attitudes.

Constantly Risking Absurdity

Constantly risking absurdity
                            and death
            whenever he performs
                        above the heads
                                    of his audience
    the poet like an acrobat
                        climbs on rime
                        to a high wire of his own making
    and balancing on eyebeams
                        above a sea of faces
            paces his way
                    to the other side of day
        performing entrechats
                    and sleight-of-foot tricks
    and other high theatrics
                        and all without mistaking
            any thing
                    for what it may not be

        For he's the super realist
                        who must perforce perceive
            taut truth
                        before the taking of each stance or
                                                step
        in his supposed advance
                        toward that still higher perch
    where Beauty stands and waits
                        with gravity
                            to start her death-defying
                                            leap

And he
a little charleychaplin man
who may or may not catch
her fair eternal form
spreadeagled in the empty air
of existence

LAWRENCE FERLINGHETTI

The Maker

So he said then: I will make the poem,
I will make it now. He took pencil,
The mind's cartridge, and blank paper,
And drilled his thoughts to the slow beat

Of the blood's drum; and there it formed
On the white surface and went marching
Onward through time, while the spent cities
And dry hearts smoked in its wake.

R. S. THOMAS

Jordan II

When first my lines of heaven'ly joyes made mention,
Such was their lustre, they did so excell,
That I sought out quaint words, and trim invention;
My thoughts began to burnish, sprout, and swell,
Curling with metaphors a plain intention,
Decking the sense, as if it were to sell.

Thousands of notions in my brain did runne,
Off'ring their service, if I were not sped:
I often blotted what I had begunne;
This was not quick enough, and that was dead.
Nothing could seem too rich to clothe the sunne,
Much lesse those joyes which trample on his head.

As flames do work and winde, when they ascend,
So did I weave myself into the sense.
But while I bustled, I might heare a friend
Whisper, *How wide is all this long pretence!*
There is in love a sweetnesse readie penn'd:
Copie out onely that, and save expense.

GEORGE HERBERT

Summary

Poetry for Supper

'Listen, now, verse should be as natural
As the small tuber that feeds on muck
And grows slowly from obtuse soil
To the white flower of immortal beauty.'

Poetry written — through magic inspiration

'Natural, hell! What was it Chaucer
Said once about the long toil
That goes like blood to the poem's making?
Leave it to nature and the verse sprawls,
Limp as bindweed, if it break at all
Life's iron crust. Man, you must sweat
And rhyme your guts taut, if you'd build
Your verse a ladder.'

        'You speak as though
No sunlight ever surprised your mind
Groping on its cloudy path.'

inspiration starts but needs work after

'Sunlight's a thing that needs a window
Before it enter a dark room.
Windows don't happen.'

        So two old poets,
Hunched at their beer in the low haze
Of an inn parlour, while the talk ran
Noisily by them, glib with prose.

R. S. THOMAS

says poetry needs a clear + planning

reads second poem

just said smooth talker using words easily without a big thought or meaning

On Being Chosen for A Schools Anthology

Mostly shame, I suppose, at inadequacies
explained away: the right rhyme chosen
for the wrong reason. And tiptoed voices
nibbling at a line which once was fact.

My own two kids could tell them: the slapped
face and the breakfast roar of the bore who sat
cuddling himself in the flat's best corner.

If the truth were known, it is nothing I have
written should be shown in a cloth book in a
cold classroom. But myself in a desk I have
not outgrown with the innocents ringed
around me – pausing as I put in my thumb,
exclaiming as I draw a plum, applauding as I make
the private joke I have in time become.

EDWIN BROCK

Afterwards

When the Present has latched its postern behind my tremulous
    stay,
And the May month flaps its glad green leaves like wings,
Delicate-filmed as new-spun silk, will the neighbours say,
    'He was a man who used to notice such things'?

If it be in the dusk when, like an eyelid's soundless blink,

The dewfall-hawk¹ comes crossing the shades to alight
Upon the wind-warped upland thorn, a gazer may think,
    'To him this must have been a familiar sight.'

If I pass during some nocturnal blackness, mothy and warm,
    When the hedgehog travels furtively over the lawn,
One may say, 'He strove that such innocent creatures should
    come to no harm,
But he could do little for them; and now he is gone.'

If, when hearing that I have been stilled at last, they stand at
    the door,
Watching the full-starred heavens that winter sees,
Will this thought rise on those who will meet my face no more,
    'He was one who had an eye for such mysteries'?

And will any say when my bell of quittance is heard in the gloom,
    And a crossing breeze cuts a pause in its outrollings,
Till they rise again, as they were a new bell's boom,
    'He hears it not now, but used to notice such things'?

THOMAS HARDY

PART B

PEOPLE

Follower

My father worked with a horse-plough,
His shoulders globed like a full sail strung
Between the shafts and the furrow.
The horses strained at his clicking tongue.

An expert. He would set the wing
And fit the bright steel-pointed sock.
The sod rolled over without breaking.
At the headrig, with a single pluck

Of reins, the sweating team turned round
And back into the land. His eye
Narrowed and angled at the ground,
Mapping the furrow exactly.

I stumbled in his hob-nailed wake,
Fell sometimes on the polished sod;
Sometimes he rode me on his back
Dipping and rising to his plod.

I wanted to grow up and plough,
To close one eye, stiffen my arm.
All I ever did was follow
In his broad shadow round the farm.

I was a nuisance, tripping, falling,
Yapping always. But today
It is my father who keeps stumbling
Behind me, and will not go away.

SEAMUS HEANEY

The Drawer

Their belongings were buried side by side
In a shallow bureau drawer. There was her
Crocodile handbag, letters, a brooch,
All that was in the bedside cupboard
And a small green jar she'd had for flowers.

My father's were in an envelope:
A khaki lanyard, crushed handkerchief,
Twelve cigarettes, a copying-pencil,
All he had on him when he was killed
Or all my mother wanted to keep.

I put them together, seven years ago.
Now that we've moved, my wife and I,
To a house of our own, I've taken them out.
Until we can find another spare drawer
They're packed in a cardboard box in the hall.

So this dead, middle-aged, middle-class man
Killed by a misfired shell, and his wife
Dead of cirrhosis, have left one son
Aged nine, aged nineteen, aged twenty-six,
Who has buried them both in a cardboard box.

GEORGE MacBETH

Death in Leamington

She died in the upstairs bedroom
　　By the light of the ev'ning star
That shone through the plate glass window
　　From over Leamington Spa.

43

Beside her the lonely crochet
    Lay patiently and unstirred,
But the fingers that would have work'd it
    Were dead as the spoken word.

And Nurse came in with the tea-things
    Breast high 'mid the stands and chairs –
But Nurse was alone with her own little soul,
    And the things were alone with theirs.

She bolted the big round window,
    She let the blinds unroll,
She set a match to the mantle,
    She covered the fire with coal.

And 'Tea!' she said in a tiny voice
    'Wake up! It's nearly five.'
Oh! Chintzy, chintzy cheeriness,
    Half dead and half alive!

Do you know that the stucco is peeling?
    Do you know that the heart will stop?
From those yellow Italianate arches
    Do you hear the plaster drop?

Nurse looked at the silent bedstead,
    At the gray, decaying face,
As the calm of a Leamington ev'ning
    Drifted into the place.

She moved the table of bottles
    Away from the bed to the wall;
And tiptoeing gently over the stairs
    Turned down the gas in the hall.

                    JOHN BETJEMAN

44

Mrs. Root

Busybody, nosey-parker
lacking the vast discretion of most
was this woman. The self-cast
chief mourner at funerals, worker
at weddings, she could sniff out death
in a doctor's optimism, joggle
a maiden's mind (button-holed on the front path)
till virginity bit like filed teeth.

Prepared, without discrimination,
friend and enemy for the grave.
Washed, talcumed them all. A woman
who wore such ceremonies like a glove,
could console a grief-struck household
that hardly knew her name, and then
collect money for a wreath fit to wield
at a Queen's passing. Death-skilled
but no less wedding-wise,
her hand stitched the perfecting dart
in bridal satin; she brought report
of cars arriving, clear skies
towards the church. They were her tears
(pew-stifled) from which the happiest
laughter billowed confetti outside the black doors.
Of best wishes, loudest were hers.

And nobody thanked her. Why doesn't
she mind her own business? they said
who'd leant upon her. Crude and peasant-like
her interest in brides, and the dead.
I thought so too, yet still was loth
to add my voice, sensing that
my secret poems were like her actions: both
pried into love and savoured death.

TONY CONNOR

45

An Old Man

Looking upon this tree with its quaint pretension
Of holding the earth, a leveret, in its claws,
Or marking the texture of its living bark,
A grey sea wrinkled by the winds of years,
I understand whence this man's body comes,
Its veins and fibres, the bare boughs of bone,
The trellised thicket, where the heart, that robin,
Greets with a song the seasons of the blood.

But where in meadow or mountain shall I match
The individual accent of the speech
That is the ear's familiar? To what sun attribute
The honey warmness of his smile?
To which of the deciduous brood is german[1]   [1]most closely
The angel peeping from the latticed eye?   related

R. S. THOMAS

The Garden

Like a skein of loose silk blown against a wall
She walks by the railing of a path
      in Kensington Gardens,
And she is dying piece-meal
      of a sort of emotional anaemia.

And round about there is a rabble
Of the filthy, sturdy, unkillable infants of the very poor.
They shall inherit the earth.

In her is the end of breeding.
Her boredom is exquisite and excessive.
She would like some one to speak to her,
And is almost afraid that I
      will commit that indiscretion.

EZRA POUND

…rtrait of his Mother, *Dürer*

Elegy for Alfred Hubbard

Hubbard is dead, the old plumber;
who will mend our burst pipes now,
the tap that has dripped all the summer,
testing the sink's overflow?

No other like him. Young men with knowledge
of new techniques, theories from books,
may better his work straight from college,
but who will challenge his squint-eyed looks

in kitchen, bathroom, under floorboards,
rules of thumb which were often wrong;
seek as erringly stopcocks in cupboards,
or make a job last half as long?

He was a man who knew the ginnels,
alleyways, streets – the whole district;
family secrets, minor annals,
time-honoured fictions fused to fact.

Seventy years of gossip muttered
under his cap, his tufty thatch,
so that his talk was slow and clotted,
hard to follow, and too much.

As though nothing fell, none vanished,
and time were the maze of Cheetham Hill,
in which the dead – with jobs unfinished –
waited to hear him ring the bell.

For much he never got round to doing,
but meant to, when the weather bucked up,
or worsened, or when his pipe was drawing,
or when he'd finished this cup.

Man with an advertising board. *Photo: Eric Schneider*

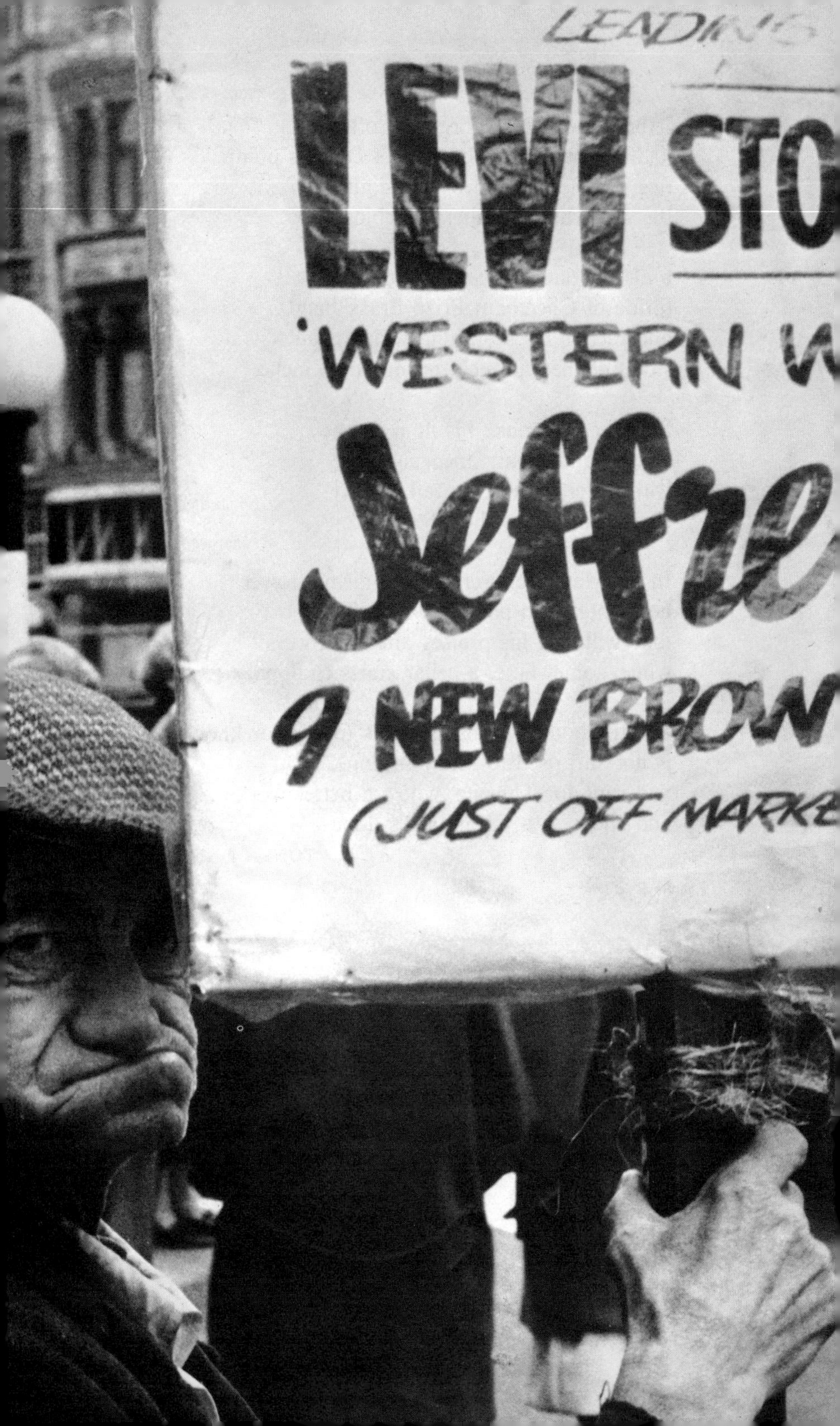
LENDIN
LEVI STO
'WESTERN W
Jeffre
9 NEW BROW
(JUST OFF MARKE

I thought time, he forgot so often,
had forgotten him, but here's Death's pomp
over his house, and by the coffin
the son who will inherit his blowlamp,

tools, workshop, cart, and cornet,
(pride of Cheetham Prize Brass Band),
and there's his mourning widow, Janet,
stood at the gate he'd promised to mend.

Soon he will make his final journey;
shaved and silent, strangely trim,
with never a pause to talk to any-
body: how arrow-like, for him!

In St. Mark's church, whose dismal tower
he pointed and painted when a lad,
they will sing his praises amidst flowers
while, somewhere, a cellar starts to flood,

and the housewife banging his front-door knocker
is not surprised to find him gone,
and runs for Thwaite, who's a better worker,
and sticks at a job until it's done.

TONY CONNOR

Docker

There, in the corner, staring at his drink.
The cap juts like a gantry's crossbeam,
Cowling plated forehead and sledgehead jaw.
Speech is clamped in the lips' vice.

That fist would drop a hammer on a Catholic –
Oh yes, that kind of thing could start again;
The only Roman collar he tolerates
Smiles all round his sleek pint of porter.

Mosaic imperatives bang home like rivets;
God is a foreman with certain definite views
Who orders life in shifts of work and leisure.
A factory horn will blare the Resurrection.

He sits, strong and blunt as a Celtic cross,
Clearly used to silence and an armchair:
Tonight the wife and children will be quiet
At slammed door and smoker's cough in the hall.

SEAMUS HEANEY

A Civil Servant

While in this cavernous place employed
    Not once was I aware
Of my officious other-self
    Poised high above me there,

My self reversed, my rage-less part,
    A slimy yellow-ish cone –
Drip, drip; drip, drip – so down the years
    I stalagmatised in stone.

Now pilgrims to the cave, who come
    To chip off what they can,
Prod me with child-like merriment:
    'Look, look! It's like a man!'

ROBERT GRAVES

51

The Clown

Circo Price, Madrid

He wears the spangled pantaloons
And swings their divided crinoline
From clever hips, where bitty rings
On blanched fingers point his quips.

A bracelet of brilliants round
One bony ankle coruscates
White stockings and pointed pumps
On slender shanks and tiny feet.

The dead-white face obliterates
All but the empty glitter of his eyes
And the thin red lips, like a tart's,
Rimming the dingy sparkle of a smile.

One huge black eyebrow, masked
In permanent inquiry, mocks
The other, significantly mean.
His questions beg the innocent reply.

His rustic companion's broad response
Is no concern of his, though he pretends surprise.
His smartness shames the heart, whose ignorance
Can ask no questions, and can tell no lies.

JAMES KIRKUP

London–Tokyo

There is no other creature like
The one fate sets beside us in a 'plane:
The vivacious grandmother, experienced traveller;
The amateur technician – 'Don't look now, but
That number four propeller seems to be fluctuating madly — ';
The convent schoolgirl mooning over Simone Weil;
The Indian mystic with his blissful flies undone;
The British maniac scribbling postcards all the night,
Counting and re-counting his collected works
That he stacks and shuffles, deals like decks of cards.

However wild a silence we may keep,
We moodily involve them in our private glooms:
We turn their glance upon the old moon lying on its back,
And wolf their breakfasts on our individual trays.
He knows 'the little boys' room' at every gritty port,
While she, 'at crazy prices', snaps up fags and lipsticks, drink
        and scent.

Reaching their several destinations, they
Matily wish us 'Happy Landings!' while we try
To smile blandly as the shuddering jet-plane takes
Its running jump at yet another sky.

                                    JAMES KIRKUP

After the Fireworks

Back into the light and warmth,
Boots clogged with mud, toes
Welded to wedges of cold flesh,
The children warm their hands on mugs
While, on remembered lawns, the flash
Of fireworks dazzles night;
Sparklers spray and rockets swish,
Soar high and break in falling showers
Of glitter; the bonfire gallivants,
Its lavish flames shimmy, prance,
And lick the straddling guy.
We wait for those great leaves of heat
And broken necklaces of light
To dim and die.
And then the children go to bed.
Tomorrow they will search the grey ground
For debris of tonight: the sad
And saturated cardboard stems,
The fallen rocket sticks, the charred
Hubs of catherine-wheels;
Then, having gathered all they've found,
They'll leave them scattered carelessly
For us to clear away.
But now the children are asleep,
And you and I sit silently
And hear, from far off in the night,
The last brave rocket burst and fade.
We taste the darkness in the light,
Reflect that fireworks are not cheap
And ask ourselves uneasily
If, even now, we've fully paid.

VERNON SCANNELL

Protest March. *Photo: Philip Jones Griffiths*

Balloons

Since Christmas they have lived with us,
Guileless and clear,
Oval soul-animals,
Taking up half the space,
Moving and rubbing on the silk

Invisible air drifts,
Giving a shriek and pop
When attacked, then scooting to rest, barely trembling.
Yellow cathead, blue fish –
Such queer moons we live with

Instead of dead furniture!
Straw mats, white walls
And these travelling
Globes of thin air, red, green,
Delighting

The heart like wishes or free
Peacocks blessing
Old ground with a feather
Beaten in starry metals.
Your small

Brother is making
His balloon squeak like a cat.
Seeming to see
A funny pink world he might eat on the other side of it,
He bites,

Then sits
Back, fat jug
Contemplating a world clear as water,
A red
Shred in his little fist.

SYLVIA PLATH

The Monk

A Monk ther was, a fair for the
   maistrie[1]   [1]an excellent one
An outridere, that lovede venerie[2],   [2]hunting
A manly man, to been an abbot able.
Ful many a deyntee[3] hors hadde he in   [3]valuable
   stable,
And whan he rood, men myghte his brydel heere
Gynglen in a whistlynge wynd als cleere
And eek as loude as dooth the chapel belle.
. . . . .
Therfore he was a prikasour[4] aright: [4]a hard galloper
Grehoundes he hadde as swift as fowel in flight;
Of prikyng and of huntyng for the hare
Was al his lust, for no cost wolde he spare.
I seigh his sleves purfiled at the hond
With grys, and that the fyneste of a lond[5]; [5]trimmed at the cuff
And, for to festne his hood under his   with costly grey fur
   chyn,
He hadde of gold ywroght a ful curious pyn;
A love-knotte in the gretter ende ther was.
His heed was balled, that shoon as any glas,
And eek his face, as he hadde been enoynt.
He was a lord ful fat and in good
   poynt[6],   [6]condition
His eyen stepe[7], and rollynge in his heed, [7]large and protruding
That stemed as a forneys of a leed[8];   [8]furnace under a
His bootes souple, his hors in greet estaat. cauldron
Now certeinly he was a fair prelaat;
He was nat pale as a forpyned[9] goost.   [9]tormented
A fat swan loved he best of any roost.
His palfrey was as broun as is a berye.

            (from the *General Prologue* to
              The Canterbury Tales)
            GEOFFREY CHAUCER

The Prioresse

Ther was also a Nonne, a PRIORESSE,
That of hir smylyng was ful symple and coy;
Hire gretteste ooth was but by Seinte Loy;
And she was cleped madame Eglentyne.
Ful weel she soong the service dyvyne,
Entuned in hir nose ful semely,
And Frenssh she spak ful faire and
        fetisly[1],   [1]elegantly
After the scole of Stratford atte Bowe,
For Frenssh of Parys was to hire unknowe.
At mete wel ytaught was she with alle:
She leet no morsel from hir lippes falle,
Ne wette hir fyngres in hir sauce depe;
Wel koude she carie a morsel and wel kepe
That no drope ne fille upon hire brest.
In curteisie was set ful muchel hir lest[2].   [2]She took great
Hir over-lippe wyped she so clene   pleasure in polite
That in hir coppe ther was no ferthyng   manners.
        sene
Of grece, whan she dronken hadde hir draughte.
Ful semely after hir mete she raught[3].   [3]reached
And sikerly she was of greet desport[4],   [4]and certainly she
And ful plesaunt, and amyable of port,   was a very cheerful
And peyned hire to countrefete cheere   person
Of court, and to been estatlich of
        manere[5],
And to ben holden digne of reverence[6].   [5]she took pains to
But, for to speken of hire conscience,   imitate courtly be-
She was so charitable and so pitous   haviour, and to be
She wolde wepe, if that she saugh a   dignified in her
        mous   bearing
Kaught in a trappe, if it were deed or bledde.   [6]held worthy

58

Of smale houndes hadde she that she fedde
With rosted flessh, or milk and wastel-
    breed[7].   [7]fine wheat bread
But soore wepte she if oon of hem were deed,
Or if men smoot it with a yerde smerte;
And al was conscience and tendre herte.
Ful semyly hir wympul[8] pynched[9] was,   [8]wimple [9]pleated
Hir nose tretys[10], hir eyen greye as glas,   [10]well shaped
Hir mouth ful smal, and thereto softe and reed;
But sikerly she hadde a fair forheed;
It was almoost a spanne brood[11], I   [11]a span broad
    trowe;
For, hardily, she was nat undergrowe.
Ful fetys was hir cloke, as I was war.
Of smal coral aboute hire arm she bar
A peire of bedes, gauded al with grene,
And theron heng a brooch of gold ful sheene,
On which ther was first write a crowned A,
And after *Amor vincit omnia*[12].   [12]Love conquers all

           (from the *General Prologue* to
             The Canterbury Tales)
           GEOFFREY CHAUCER

The Little Cart

The little cart jolting and banging through the yellow haze
    of dusk;
The man pushing behind, the woman pulling in front.
They have left the city and do not know where to go.
'Green, green, those elm-tree leaves; *they* will cure my
    hunger,
If only we could find some quiet place and sup on them
    together.'

The wind has flattened the yellow mother-wort;
Above it in the distance they see the walls of a house.
'*There* surely must be people living who'll give you something
  to eat.'
They tap at the door, but no-one comes; they look in, but
  the kitchen is empty.
They stand hesitating in the lonely road and their tears fall
  like rain.

CH'ÉN TZŬ-LUNG
(*trans. Arthur Waley*)

John Henry

*John Henry was 'a steel driving man' – a railroad worker whose task was to
drill holes in the rocks for the dynamite charges by striking the drill with a hammer.
The legend tells of a contest between John Henry and a steam drill during the
construction of the C. & O. tunnel at Big Bend, West Virginia. There are many
versions of the John Henry story and the sequence of the verses is frequently
uncertain.*

When John Henry was a little boy,
Sitting upon his father's knee,
His father said, 'Look here, my boy,
You must be a steel driving man like me,
You must be a steel driving man like me.'

John Henry had a little wife,
And the dress she wore was red;
The last thing before he died,
He said, 'Be true to me when I'm dead,
Oh, be true to me when I'm dead.'

John Henry's wife ask him for fifteen cents,
And he said he didn't have but a dime,
Said, 'If you wait till the rising sun goes down,
I'll borrow it from the man in the mine,
I'll borrow it from the man in the mine.'

John Henry went upon the mountain,
Just to drive himself some steel.
The rocks were so tall and John Henry so small,
He said lay down hammer and squeal,
He said lay down hammer and squeal.

John Henry started on the right-hand side,
And the steam drill started on the left.
He said, 'Before I'd let that steam drill beat me down,
I'd hammer my fool self to death,
Oh, I'd hammer my fool self to death.'

The steam drill started at half past six,
John Henry started the same time.
John Henry struck bottom at half past eight,
And the steam drill didn't bottom till nine,
And the steam drill didn't bottom till nine.

John Henry said to his captain,
'A man, he ain't nothing but a man,
Before I'd let that steam drill beat me down,
I'd die with the hammer in my hand,
Oh, I'd die with the hammer in my hand.'

John Henry said to his shaker,
'Shaker, why don't you sing just a few more rounds?
And before the setting sun goes down,
You're gonna hear this hammer of mine sound,
You're gonna hear this hammer of mine sound.'

John Henry hammered on the mountain,
He hammered till half past three,
He said, 'This big Bend Tunnel on the C. & O. road
Is going to be the death of me,
Lord! is going to be the death of me.'

John Henry had a little baby boy,
You could hold him in the palm of your hand.
The last words before he died,
'Son, you must be a steel driving man,
Son, you must be a steel driving man.'

John Henry had a little woman,
And the dress she wore was red,
She went down the railroad track and never come back,
Said she was going where John Henry fell dead,
Said she was going where John Henry fell dead.

John Henry hammering on the mountain,
As the whistle blew for half past two,
The last word I heard him say,
'Captain, I've hammered my insides in two,
Lord, I've hammered my insides in two.'

collected GUY B. JOHNSON

Rugby League Game

Sport is absurd, and sad.
Those grown men, just look,
In those dreary long blue shorts,
Those ringed stockings, Edwardian,
Balding pates, and huge
Fat knees that ought to be heroes'.

Grappling, hooking, gallantly tackling –
Is all this courage really necessary? –
Taking their good clean fun
So solemnly, they run each other down
With earnest keenness, for the honour of
Virility, the cap, the county side.

The Runners, *R. Delaunay*

Like great boys they roll each other
In the mud of public Saturdays,
Groping their blind way back
To noble youth, away from the bank,
The wife, the pram, the spin drier,
Back to the spartan freedom of the field.

Back, back to the days when boys
Were men, still hopeful, and untamed.
That was then: a gay
And golden age ago.
Now, in vain, domesticated,
Men try to be boys again.

JAMES KIRKUP

Creative Writing

1 The two poems on pp. 42 and 43 are written from the point of view of a son.

What do you really *feel* and think about your parents?

Jot down five or six ways in which you have been made aware of *your* feelings for one or both parents (these may be particular incidents or recurring feelings).

In what ways can you see yourself in one or other of your parents? Appearance? Mannerisms? Temperament? Interests?

What are the biggest differences between you and them? After you have discussed some of these points amongst yourselves you may find that you have ideas for a piece of original writing.

2 All families row and argue at some time: feelings of immense fury, exasperation, frustration often arise over trivial things. Try to describe your feelings after a family row.

3 Boredom is something we all feel from time to time: perhaps you are feeling it now. How do you behave when you are bored? What sort of things take your eye when you look around? What do you think about? How do you occupy your hands when bored? Try to list the details which are symptoms of your boredom: there might be a poem here.

4 Write a poem entitled 'Me'. Ask yourself how you appear to yourself and to others. Are the two pictures the same?

5 If you could be someone else, who would you choose to be? A popular hero of T.V., film, football or 'pop' music or someone less in the public eye? Perhaps you could write about your ideal.

6 The pictures on pp. 47 and 49 are both of elderly people and, although one is a modern photograph and the other a sixteenth-century drawing, it is worth considering in what ways they are similar. What tells you they are old? What physical details do you notice? Write a poem about old age either by trying to visualise an elderly person, real or imaginary, or by using one of these pictures.

7 The pictures on pp. 55 and 63 both concern youth. R. Delaunay's *The Runners* catches the feeling of individual athletes competing against each other. It may suggest to you an idea for a piece of writing connected with a sport which you enjoy. The photograph of the protest marchers has many of the trappings we associate with

demonstrations – badges, guitars, emotive placards and banners. How do you react? Do you want to join these young people or do you think that they are wasting their time? Perhaps you could write a poem suggested by the picture.

RELIGIOUS EXPERIENCE

Woefully Arrayed

Woefully arrayed,
  My blood, man,
  For thee ran,
It may not be naid[1];   [1]denied
  My body blue and wan,
Woefully arrayed.

Behold me, I pray thee, with all thy whole reason,
And be not so hard-hearted, and for this encheson[2],   [2]reason
Sith I for thy soul sake was slain in good season,
Beguiled and betrayed by Judas' false treason;
    Unkindly entreatèd,
    With sharp cord sore frettèd,
    The Jewis me threatèd,
They mowèd[3], they grinnèd, they scornèd me,   [3]sneered
Condemnèd to death, as thou mayest see,
Woefully arrayed.

Thus naked am I nailèd, O man, for thy sake!
I love thee, then love me; why sleepest thou? awake!
Remember my tender heart root for thee brake,
With pains my veins constrainèd to crake;
    Thus tuggèd to and fro,
    Thus wrappèd all in woe,
    Whereas never man was so,
Entreatèd thus in most cruel wise,
Was like a lamb offered in sacrifice,
Woefully arrayed.

Of sharp thorn I have worn a crown on my head
So painèd, so strainèd, so rueful, so red;

Thus bobbèd[4], thus robbèd, thus for thy love dead, [4]mocked
Unfeignèd not deignèd my blood for to shed;
    My feet and handès sore
    The sturdy nails bore;
    What might I suffer more
    Than I have done, O man, for thee?
  Come when thou list, welcome to me,
    Woefully arrayed.

Of record thy good Lord I have been and shall be;
I am thine, thou art mine, my brother I call thee;
Thee love I entirely; see what is befall'n me!
Sore beating, sore threating, to make thee, man, all free:
    Why art thou unkind?
    Why hast not me in mind?
    Come yet and thou shalt find
  Mine endless mercy and grace;
  See how a spear my heart did race,
    Woefully arrayed.

Dear brother, no other thing I of thee desire
But give me thine heart free to reward mine hire:
I wrought thee, I bought thee from eternal fire;
I pray thee array thee toward my high empire
    Above the orient,
    Whereof I am regent,
    Lord God omnipotent,
  With me to reign in endless wealth;
  Remember, man, thy soul's health.

    Woefully arrayed
      My blood, man,
      For thee ran,
    It may not be naid;
      My body blue and wan,
    Woefully arrayed.

JOHN SKELTON

Pied Beauty

Glory be to God for dappled things –
   For skies of couple-colour as a brinded cow;
      For rose-moles all in stipple upon trout that swim;
Fresh-firecoal chestnut-falls; finches' wings;
   Landscape plotted and pieced – fold, fallow, and plough;
      And áll trádes, their gear and tackle and trim.
All things counter, original, spare, strange;
   Whatever is fickle, freckled (who knows how?)
      With swift, slow; sweet, sour; adazzle, dim;
He fathers-forth whose beauty is past change:
         Praise him.

GERARD MANLEY HOPKINS

Vertue

Sweet day, so cool, so calm, so bright,
The bridall of the earth and skie:
The dew shall weep thy fall to night;
      For thou must die.

Sweet rose, whose hue angrie and brave
Bids the rash gazer wipe his eye:
Thy root is ever in its grave,
      And thou must die.

Sweet spring, full of sweet dayes and roses,
A box where sweets[1] compacted lie;   [1]perfumes
My musick shows ye have your closes,
      And all must die.

Onely a sweet and vertuous soul,
Like season'd timber, never gives;
But though the whole world turn to coal,
      Then chiefly lives.

GEORGE HERBERT

Love (III)

Love bade me welcome: yet my soul drew back,
        Guiltie of dust and sinne.
But quick-ey'd Love, observing me grow slack
        From my first entrance in,
Drew nearer to me, sweetly questioning.
        If I lack'd anything.

A guest, I answer'd, worthy to be here:
        Love said, You shall be he.
I the unkinde, ungratefull? Ah my deare,
        I cannot look on thee.
Love took my hand, and smiling did reply,
        Who made the eyes but I?

Truth Lord, but I have marr'd them: let my shame
        Go where it doth deserve.
And know you not, sayes Love, who bore the blame?
        My deare, then I will serve.
You must sit down, says Love, and taste my meat:
        So I did sit and eat.

GEORGE HERBERT

I Have Not Seen God

I have not seen God face to face
Therefore I cannot fear Him
But I fear lightning and the anger of righteous men,
And this grasping at space
In a night grown huge behind the trembling stars.

69

I have not seen God face to face
Therefore I cannot worship Him
But I worship mountains that wear a bloom of grapes
In the evening sun; I worship primitive things —
Trees and essential shapes
Of beauty outlined in the world we touch.

I have not seen God face to face
Therefore I cannot love Him
But I love the light that quickens wood and stone,
The sudden grace
Lifting a dull pedestrian out of time
And place, to find the Unknown through the known.

PHOEBE HESKETH

Spring

Nothing is so beautiful as spring —
   When weeds, in wheels, shoot long and lovely and lush;
   Thrush's eggs look little low heavens, and thrush
Through the echoing timber does so rinse and wring
The ear, it strikes like lightnings to hear him sing;
   The glassy peartree leaves and blooms, they brush
   The descending blue; that blue is all in a rush
With richness; the racing lambs too have fair their fling.

What is all this juice and all this joy?
   A strain of the earth's sweet being in the beginning
In Eden garden. — Have, get, before it cloy,
   Before it cloud, Christ, lord, and sour with sinning,
Innocent mind and Mayday in girl and boy,
   Most, O maid's child, thy choice and worthy the winning.

GERARD MANLEY HOPKINS

Upon a Dead Man's Head

Your ugly token
My mind hath broken
From worldly lust:
For I have discust
We are but dust,
And die we must.

   It is general
To be mortal:
I have well espied
No man may him hide
From Death hollow-eyed,
With sinews wyderèd[1],   [1]withered
With bones shyderèd,
With his worm-eaten maw,
And his ghastly jaw
Gasping aside,
Naked of hide,
Neither flesh nor fell.

   Then, by my counsel,
Look that ye spell
Well this gospel:
For whereso we dwell
Death will us quell,
And with us mell.

   For all our pampered paunches
There may no fraunchis[2],   [2]privilege or liberality
Nor worldly bliss,
Redeem us from this:
Our days be dated
To be checkmated
With draughtes of death
Stopping our breath:
Our eyen sinking,
Our bodies stinking,

71

Our gummes grinning,
Our soules brinning[3].   [3]burning
To whom, then, shall we sue,
For to have rescue,
But to sweet Jesu
On us then for to rue[4]?   [4]be sorry
   O goodly Child
Of Mary mild,
Then be our shield!
That we be not exiled
To the dyne[5] dale   [5]noisy
Of bootless bale[6],   [6]torment
Nor to the lake
Of fiendes black.
   But grant us grace
To see thy Face,
And to purchase
Thine heavenly place,
And thy palace
Full of solace
Above the sky
That is so high;
Eternally
To behold and see
The Trinity!
   Amen.

JOHN SKELTON

Christ Climbed Down

Christ climbed down
from His bare Tree
this year
and ran away to where
there were no rootless Christmas trees
hung with candycanes and breakable stars

Christ climbed down
from His bare Tree
this year
and ran away to where
there were no gilded Christmas trees
and no tinsel Christmas trees
and no tinfoil Christmas trees
and no pink plastic Christmas trees
and no gold Christmas trees
and no black Christmas trees
and no powderblue Christmas trees
hung with electric candles
and encircled by tin electric trains
and clever cornball relatives

Christ climbed down
from His bare Tree
this year
and ran away to where
no intrepid Bible salesmen
covered the territory
in two-tone cadillacs
and where no Sears Roebuck creches
completed with plastic babe in manger
arrived by parcel post
the babe by very special delivery
and where no televised Wise Men
praised the Lord Calvert Whiskey

Christ climbed down
from His bare Tree
this year
and ran away to where
no fat handshaking stranger
in a red flannel suit
and a fake white beard
went around passing himself off

73

as some sort of North Pole saint
crossing the desert to Bethlehem
Pennsylvania
in a Volkswagen sled
drawn by rollicking Adirondack reindeer
with German names
and bearing sacks of Humble Gifts
from Saks Fifth Avenue
for everybody's imagined Christ child

Christ climbed down
from His bare Tree
this year
and ran away to where
no Bing Crosby carollers
groaned of a tight Christmas
and where no Radio City angels
iceskated wingless
thru a winter wonderland
into a jinglebell heaven
daily at 8:30
with Midnight Mass matinees

Christ climbed down
from His bare Tree
this year
and softly stole away into
some anonymous Mary's womb again
where in the darkest night
of everybody's anonymous soul
He awaits again
an unimaginable
and impossibly
Immaculate Reconception
the very craziest
of Second Comings

LAWRENCE FERLINGHETTI

After Christmas

Gone is that errant star. The shepherds rise
And, packed in buses, go their separate ways
To bench and counter where their flocks will graze
On winter grass, no bonus of sweet hay.
The myrrh, the frankincense fade from memory:
Another year of waiting for the day.

Still in his palace Herod waits for orders:
Arrests, an edict, more judicial murders,
New taxes, reinforcements for the borders.
Still high priests preach decorum, rebels rage
At Caesar battening on their heritage
And a few prophets mourn a godless age.

The Magi in three chauffeur-driven cars
Begin their homeward journey round the wars,
Each to his capital, the stocks and shares
Whose constellations, flickering into place,
Must guide him through a vaster wilderness
Than did the star absconded out of space.

The golden thread winds back upon the spool.
A bird's dry carcass and an empty bottle
Beside the dustbin, vomit of goodwill,
Pale streets, pale faces and a paler sky;
A paper Bethlehem, a rootless tree
Soon to be stripped, dismembered, put away,

Burnt on the grate . . . and dressed in candlelight
When next the shepherds turn their flocks about,
The three wise kings recall their second state
And from the smaller circle of the year,
Axle and weighted hub, look high and far
To pierce their weekday heaven that hides the star.

MICHAEL HAMBURGER

Christmas Shopping

Spending beyond their income on gifts for Christmas –
Swing doors and crowded lifts and draperied jungles –
What shall we buy for our husbands and sons
    Different from last year?

Foxes hang by their noses behind plate glass –
Scream of macaws across festoons of paper –
Only the faces on the boxes of chocolates are free
    From boredom and crowsfeet.

Sometimes a chocolate-box girl escapes in the flesh,
Lightly manœuvres the crowd, trilling with laughter;
After a couple of years her feet and her brain will
    Tire like the others.

The great windows marshal their troops for assault on the purse
Something-and-eleven the yard, hoodwinking logic,
The eleventh hour draining the gurgling pennies
    Down to the conduits

Down to the sewers of money – rats and marshgas –
Bubbling in maundering music under the pavement;
Here go the hours of routine, the weight on our eyelids –
    Pennies on corpses.

While over the street in the centrally heated public
Library dwindling figures with sloping shoulders
And hands in pockets, weighted in the boots like chessmen,
    Stare at the printed

Columns of ads, the quickest road to riches,
Starting at a little and temporary but once we're
Started who knows whether we shan't continue,
    Salaries rising,

Rising like a salmon against the bullnecked river,
Bound for the spawning-ground of care-free days –
Good for a fling before the golden wheels run
   Down to a standstill.

And Christ is born. – The nursery glad with baubles,
Alive with light and washable paint and children's
Eyes, expects as its due to the accidental
   Loot of a system.

Smell of the South – oranges in silver paper,
Dates and ginger, the benison of firelight,
The blue flames dancing round the brandied raisins,
   Smiles from above them,

Hands from above them as of gods but really
These their parents, always seen from below, them-
Selves are always anxious looking across the
   Fence to the future –

Out there lies the future gathering quickly
Its blank momentum; through the tubes of London
The dead winds blow the crowds like beasts in flight from
   Fire in the forest.

The little firtrees palpitate with candles
In hundreds of chattering households where the suburb
Straggles like nervous handwriting, the margin
   Blotted with smokestacks.

Further out on the coast the lighthouse moves its
Arms of light through the fog that wads our welfare,
Moves its arms like a giant at Swedish drill whose
   Mind is a vacuum.

                  LOUIS MacNEICE

Water

If I were called in
To construct a religion
I should make use of water.

Going to church
Would entail a fording
To dry, different clothes;

My litany would employ
Images of sousing,
A furious devout drench,

And I should raise in the east
A glass of water
Where any-angled light
Would congregate endlessly.

PHILIP LARKIN

I Felt a Funeral in My Brain

I felt a Funeral, in my Brain,
And Mourners to and fro
Kept treading – treading – till it seemed
That Sense was breaking through –

And when they all were seated,
A Service, like a Drum –
Kept beating – beating – till I thought
My Mind was going numb –

And then I heard them lift a Box
And creak across my Soul
With those same Boots of Lead, again,
Then space – began to toll,

As all the Heavens were a Bell,
And Being, but an Ear,
And I, and Silence, some strange Race
Wrecked, solitary here –

And then a Plank in Reason, broke,
And I dropped down, and down –
And hit a World, at every plunge,
And Finished knowing – then –

EMILY DICKINSON

Forgive, O Lord

Forgive, O Lord, my little jokes on Thee
And I'll forgive Thy great big one on me.

ROBERT FROST

Creative Writing

Religion is obviously something very personal and many of you will have experienced it in completely different ways. Some of you will believe in a particular faith; others will have no faith at all. Your religious attitudes, or absence of them, are basically the result of your upbringing and the society in which you live, but many of you may well be at the stage of thinking about religious beliefs for yourselves. Writing about the subject is, perhaps, one of the most useful ways of sorting out your own ideas.

1 Try to put into words your feelings during a particular religious service or ceremony you remember, for example, a wedding, your first communion, a funeral, a christening, or a major religious festival such as Christmas or Easter. What does it mean to you? to most people? How does such a service appear to you if you are not a religious person?

2 Christmas suggests different things to different people, as the group of poems following p. 72 shows. You may find it useful to discuss the attitudes which these poets have, before going on to write about your own idea of Christmas.

3 Many people, particularly teenagers, find traditional prayers and hymns dull and irrelevant. Try to up-date these by writing a modern prayer or hymn of your own which shows an awareness of present-day attitudes and problems.

4 Perhaps you could write about your own place of worship and its atmosphere, or about your feelings for one of the particularly impressive cathedrals which you may have visited where music, stained glass, carving in wood and stone all combine to give the place its special atmosphere.

5 Try to write a poem beginning with the words 'My religion is . . .' in which you list the things in life which really matter to you, whether or not they are anything to do with a formal religious belief.

6 Whether you have a faith or not there are sure to be things which you dislike about religion and about certain people who profess to be religious. After discussing some of these ideas you may have material for a poem.

TOWN AND COUNTRY

Voices from Things Growing in a Churchyard

These flowers are I, poor Fanny Hurd,
      Sir or Madam,
A little girl here sepultured.
Once I flit-fluttered like a bird
Above the grass, as now I wave
In daisy shapes above my grave,
      All day cheerily,
      All night eerily!

– I am one Bachelor Bowring, 'Gent',
      Sir or Madam,
In shingled oak my bones were pent;
Hence more than a hundred years I spent
In my feat of change from a coffin-thrall
To a dancer in green as leaves on a wall,
      All day cheerily,
      All night eerily!

– I, these berries of juice and gloss,
      Sir or Madam,
Am clean forgotten as Thomas Voss;
Thin-urned, I have burrowed away from the moss
That covers my sod, and have entered this yew,
And turned to clusters ruddy of view,
      All day cheerily,
      All night eerily!

– The Lady Gertrude, proud, high-bred,
      Sir or Madam,
Am I – this laurel that shades your head;
Into its veins I have stilly sped,
And made them of me; and my leaves now shine,
    As did my satins superfine,
      All day cheerily,
      All night eerily!

– I, who as innocent withwind[1] climb,   [1]bindweed
      Sir or Madam,
Am one Eve Greensleeves, in olden time
Kissed by men from many a clime,
Beneath sun, stars, in blaze, in breeze,
As now by glowworms and by bees,
      All day cheerily,
      All night eerily!

– I'm old Squire Audeley Grey, who grew,
      Sir or Madam,
Aweary of life, and in scorn withdrew;
Till anon I clambered up anew
As ivy-green, when my ache was stayed,
And in that attire I have longtime gayed,
      All day cheerily,
      All night eerily!

– And so these maskers breathe to each
      Sir or Madam,
Who lingers there, and their lively speech
Affords an interpreter much to teach,
As their murmurous accents seem to come
Thence hitheraround in a radiant hum,
      All day cheerily,
      All night eerily!

THOMAS HARDY

Shortest Day, 1942

For N.W.

The damp December light
Settles like fog on roofs
And gable-ends of slate;
The wind blows holes in the sky; the rain
Shines on the road like tin,
And rain-drops hang on the privet, round and white.

Behind a freestone wall,
Between the houses and the street,
In twelve or less square feet
Of tarmac and black soil
Blooms the purple primula
Bright as a lollipop or an aniseed ball.

And so a smile will flower,
A kiss like a child's laugh, or more
Like a friendly terrier's bark,
While the town huddles beneath a dark
Drizzle of misery, and the wind
Flings down sleet from the frozen fells of war.

NORMAN NICHOLSON

February Fill-Dyke, *B. W. Leader, R.A.*

November

The month of the drowned dog. After long rain the land
Was sodden as the bed of an ancient lake,
Treed with iron and birdless. In the sunk lane
The ditch — a seep silent all summer —

Made brown foam with a big voice; that, and my boots
On the lane's scrubbed stones, in the gulleyed leaves,
Against the hill's hanging silence;
Mist silvering the droplets on the bare thorns

Slower than the change of daylight.
In a let of the ditch a tramp was bundled asleep:
Face tucked down into beard, drawn in
Under its hair like a hedgehog's. I took him for dead,

But his stillness separated from the death
Of the rotting grass and the ground. A wind chilled,
And a fresh comfort tightened through him,
Each hand stuffed deeper into the other sleeve.

His ankles, bound with sacking and hairy band,
Rubbed each other, resettling. The wind hardened;
A puff shook a glittering from the thorns,
And again the rain's dragging grey columns

Smudged the farms. In a moment
The fields were jumping and smoking; the thorns
Quivering, riddled with the glassy verticals.
I stayed on under the welding cold

Watching the tramp's face glisten and the drops on his coat
Flash and darken. I thought what strong trust
Slept in him — as the trickling furrows slept,
And the thorn-roots in their grip on darkness;

And the buried stones, taking the weight of winter;
The hill where the hare crouched with clenched teeth.
Rain plastered the land till it was shining
Like hammered lead, and I ran, and in the rushing wood

Shuttered by a black oak leaned.
The keeper's gibbet had owls and hawks
By the neck, weasels, a gang of cats, crows:
Some, stiff, weightless, twirled like dry bark bits

In the drilling rain. Some still had their shape,
Had their pride with it; hung, chins on chests,
Patient to outwait these worst days that beat
Their crowns bare and dripped from their feet.

TED HUGHES

Orchids

They lean over the path,
Adder-mouthed,
Swaying close to the face,
Coming out, soft and deceptive,
Limp and damp, delicate as a young bird's tongue;
Their fluttery fledgeling lips
Move slowly,
Drawing in the warm air.

And at night,
The faint moon falling through whitewashed glass,
The heat going down
So their musky smell comes even stronger,
Drifting down from their mossy cradles:
So many devouring infants!
Soft luminescent fingers,
Lips neither dead nor alive,
Loose ghostly mouths
Breathing.

THEODORE ROETHKE

The Large Piece of Turf. *Dürer*

Soil

A field with tall hedges and a young
Moon in the branches and one star
Declining westward set the scene
Where he works slowly astride the rows
Of red mangolds and green swedes
Plying mechanically his cold blade.
This is his world, the hedge defines
The mind's limits; only the sky
Is boundless, and he never looks up;
His gaze is deep in the dark soil,
As are his feet. The soil is all;
His hands fondle it, and his bones
Are formed out of it with the swedes.
And if sometimes the knife errs,
Burying itself in his shocked flesh,
Then out of the wound the blood seeps home
To the warm soil from which it came.

R. S. THOMAS

Waterfall

The burn drowns steadily in its own downpour,
A helter-skelter of muslin and glass
That skids to a halt, crashing up suds.

Simultaneous acceleration
And sudden braking; water goes over
Like villains dropped screaming to justice.

It appears an athletic glacier
Has reared into reverse: is swallowed up
And regurgitated through this long throat.

My eye rides over and downwards, falls with
Hurtling tons that slabber and spill,
Falls, yet records the tumult thus standing still.

SEAMUS HEANEY

Sunken Evening

The green light floods the city square —
A sea of fowl and feathered fish,
Where squalls of rainbirds dive and splash
And gusty sparrows chop the air.

Submerged, the prawn-blue pigeons feed
In sandy grottoes round the Mall,
And crusted lobster-buses crawl
Among the fountains' silver weed.

There, like a wreck, with mast and bell,
The torn church settles by the bow,
While phosphorescent starlings stow
Their mussel shells along the hull.

The oyster-poet, drowned but dry,
Rolls a black pearl between his bones;
The typist, trapped by telephones,
Gazes in bubbles at the sky.

Till, with the dark, the shallows run,
And homeward surges tide and fret —
The slow night trawls its heavy net
And hauls the clerk to Surbiton.

LAURIE LEE

Stormy Day

O look how the long loops and balloons of bloom
Bobbing on long strings from the finger-ends
And knuckles of the lurching cherry-tree
Heap and hug, elbow and part, this wild day,
Like a careless carillon cavorting;
And beaded whips of beeches splay
And dip like anchored weed round a drowned rock,
And hovering effortlessly the rooks
Hang on the wind's effrontery as if
On hooks, then loose their hold and slide away
Like sleet sideways down the warm swimming sweep
Of wind. O it is a lovely time when
Out of the sunk and rigid sumps of thought
Our hearts rise and race with new sounds and sights
And signs, tingling delightedly at the sting
And crunch of springless carts on gritty roads,
The caught kite dangling in the skinny wires,
The swipe of a swallow across the eyes,
Striped awnings stretched on lawns. New things surprise
And stop us everywhere. In the parks
The fountains scoop and flower like rockets
Over the oval ponds whose even skin
Is pocked and goosefleshed by their niggling rain
That frocks a naked core of statuary.
And at jetty's jut, roped and ripe for hire,
The yellow boats lie yielding and lolling,
Jilted and jolted like jellies. But look!
There! Do you see, crucified on palings,
Motionless news-posters announcing
That now the frozen armies melt and meet
And smash? Go home now, for, try as you may,
You will not shake off that fact today.
Behind you limps that dog with tarry paw,
As behind him, perfectly timed, follows
The dumb shadow that mimes him all the way.

                                    W. R. RODGERS

Storm on the Island

We are prepared: we build our houses squat,
Sink walls in rock and roof them with good slate.
This wizened earth has never troubled us
With hay, so, as you see, there are no stacks
Or stooks that can be lost. Nor are there trees
Which might prove company when it blows full
Blast: you know what I mean — leaves and branches
Can raise a tragic chorus in a gale
So that you listen to the thing you fear
Forgetting that it pummels your house too.
But there are no trees, no natural shelter.
You might think that the sea is company,
Exploding comfortably down on the cliffs
But no: when it begins, the flung spray hits
The very windows, spits like a tame cat
Turned savage. We just sit tight while wind dives
And strafes invisibly. Space is a salvo,
We are bombarded by the empty air.
Strange, it is a huge nothing that we fear.

SEAMUS HEANEY

Portrait of a Machine

What nudity as beautiful as this
Obedient monster purring at its toil;
Those naked iron muscles dripping oil,
And the sure-fingered rods that never miss?
This long and shining flank of metal is
Magic that greasy labour cannot spoil;
While this vast engine that could rend the soil
Conceals its fury with a gentle hiss.

92

It does not vent its loathing, it does not turn
Upon its makers with destroying hate.
It bears a deeper malice; lives to earn
Its master's bread and laughs to see this great
Lord of the earth, who rules but cannot learn,
Become the slave of what his slaves create.

LOUIS UNTERMEYER

The Pylons

The secret of these hills was stone, and cottages
Of that stone made,
And crumbling roads
That turned on sudden hidden villages.

Now over these small hills, they have built the concrete
That trails black wire;
Pylons, those pillars
Bare like nude giant girls that have no secret.

The valley with its gilt and evening look
And the green chestnut
Of customary root,
Are mocked dry like the parched bed of a brook.

But far above and far as sight endures
Like whips of anger
With lightning's danger
There runs the quick perspective of the future.

This dwarfs our emerald country by its trek
So tall with prophecy:
Dreaming of cities
Where often clouds shall lean their swan-white neck.

STEPHEN SPENDER

The Place's Fault

Once, after a rotten day at school —
Sweat on my fingers, pages thumbed with smears,
Cane smashing down to make me keep them neat —
I blinked out to the sunlight and the heat
And stumbled up the hill, still swallowing tears.
A stone hissed past my ear — 'Yah! gurt fat fool!'

Some urchins waited for me by my gate.
I shouted swear-words at them, walked away.
'Yeller,' they yelled, 'e's yeller!' And they flung
Clods, stones, bricks — anything to make me run.
I ran, all right, up hill all summer day
With 'yeller' in my ears. 'I'm not, I'm not!'

Another time, playing too near the shops —
Oddly, no doubt, I'm told I was quite odd,
Making, no doubt, a noise — a girl in slacks
Came out and told some kids 'Run round the back,
Bash in his back door, smash up his back yard,
And if he yells I'll go and fetch the cops.'

And what a rush I had to lock those doors
Before that rabble reached them! What desire
I've had these twenty years to lock away
That place where fingers pointed out my play,
Where even the grass was tangled with barbed wire,
Where through the streets I waged continual wars!

We left (it was a temporary halt)
The knots of ragged kids, the wired-off beach,
Faces behind the blinds. I'll not return;
There's nothing there I haven't had to learn,
And I've learned nothing that I'd care to teach —
Except that I know it was the place's fault.

PHILIP HOBSBAUM

94

Wet roofs.   *Photo: Bill Brandt*

The Wiper

Through purblind night the wiper
Reaps a swathe of water
On the screen; we shudder on
    And hardly hold the road,
All we can see a segment
Of blackly shining asphalt
With the wiper moving across it
    Clearing, blurring, clearing.

But what to say of the road?
The monotony of its hardly
Visible camber, the mystery
    Of its far invisible margins,
Will these be always with us,
The night being broken only
By lights that pass or meet us
    From others in moving boxes?

Boxes of glass and water,
Upholstered, equipped with dials
Professing to tell the distance
We have gone, the speed we are going,
But never a gauge nor needle
To tell us where we are going
Or when day will come, supposing
    This road exists in daytime.

For now we cannot remember
Where we were when it was not
Night, when it was not raining,
    Before this car moved forward
And the wiper backward and forward
Lighting so little before us
Of a road that, crouching forward,
    We watch move always towards us,

96

Which through the tiny segment
Cleared and blurred by the wiper
Is sucked in under the axle
    To be spewed behind us and lost
While we, dazzled by darkness,
Haul the black future towards us
Peeling the skin from our hands;
    And yet we hold the road.

                    LOUIS MacNEICE

The Crane

That insect, without antennae, over its
Cotton-spool lip, letting
An almost invisible tenuity
Of steel cable, drop
Some seventy feet, with the
Grappling hook hidden also
Behind a dense foreground
Among which it is fumbling, and
Over which, mantis-like
It is begging or threatening, gracile
From a clear sky – that paternal
Constructive insect, without antennae,
Would seem to assure us that
'The future is safe, because
It is in my hands.' And we do not
Doubt this veracity, we can only
Fear it – as many of us
As pause here to remark
Such silent solicitude
For lifting intangible weights
Into real walls.

            CHARLES TOMLINSON

The Forge

All I know is a door into the dark.
Outside, old axles and iron hoops rusting;
Inside, the hammered anvil's short-pitched ring,
The unpredictable fantail of sparks
Or hiss when a new shoe toughens in water.
The anvil must be somewhere in the centre,
Horned as a unicorn, at one end square,
Set there immovable: an altar
Where he expends himself in shape and music.
Sometimes, leather-aproned, hairs in his nose,
He leans out on the jamb, recalls a clatter
Of hoofs where traffic is flashing in rows;
Then grunts and goes in, with a slam and flick
To beat real iron out, to work the bellows.

SEAMUS HEANEY

Telephone Poles

They have been with us a long time.
They will outlast the elms.
Our eyes, like the eyes of a savage sieving the trees
In his search for game,
Run through them. They blend along small-town streets
Like a race of giants that have faded into mere mythology.
Our eyes, washed clean of belief,
Lift incredulous to their fearsome crowns of bolts, trusses,
    struts, nuts, insulators, and such
Barnacles as compose
These weathered encrustations of electrical debris –
Each a Gorgon's head, which, seized right,
Could stun us to stone.

Frost on a window. *Photo: C. O'Gorman*

Yet they are ours. We made them.
See here, where the cleats of linemen
Have roughened a second bark
Onto the bald trunk. And these spikes
Have been driven sideways at intervals handy for human legs.
The Nature of our construction is in every way
A better fit than the Nature it displaces.
What other tree can you climb where the birds' twitter,
Unscrambled, is English? True, their thin shade is negligible,
But then again there is not that tragic autumnal
Casting-off of leaves to outface annually.
These giants are more constant than evergreens
By being never green.

JOHN UPDIKE

Bendix

This porthole overlooks a sea
Forever falling from the sky,
The water inextricably
Involved with buttons, suds and dye.

Like bits of shrapnel, shards of foam
Fly heavenward; a bedsheet heaves,
A stocking wrestles with a comb,
And cotton angels wave their sleeves.

The boiling purgatorial tide
Revolves our dreary shorts and slips,
While Mother coolly bakes beside
Her little jugged apocalypse.

JOHN UPDIKE

Creative Writing

1 At some time in your life you may well have moved house. Discuss
with the class what your feelings were as you left your old home
and saw your furniture stowed away in the removal van. What did
you feel about the empty house? Were there any signs that it was
once yours? What did you miss most?

How did you regard your new house, new school, new neigh-
bours?

Perhaps you could write something about either moving from
your old house or coming to live in a new area.

2 Try to write about the place which you enjoy going to most with
your friends – perhaps a coffee bar or youth-club, a dance, a pop-
concert, a cinema, a jazz-club or a football match. Concentrate
on the details which give the place its special atmosphere.

3 Those of you who have spent some time in hospital will know that
these places have an atmosphere quite unlike anywhere else.
Discuss what details produce this. Try to recall the antiseptic
smell, the clinical appearance of the ward and its staff, the unusual,
often frightening, machines and equipment, visiting time and all
the other things that make up the routine of a hospital day. There
may be a poem here.

4 If you have a room of your own, what makes it particularly yours?
Perhaps you could write about it.

5 A number of the poems in this section are about machines. You
may be able to write about a machine which you have watched in
operation – a motor bike, a lathe, a sewing machine, a washing
machine, a bull-dozer, a crane, a railway engine. Try to make the
line lengths, word-sounds and comparisons suit the details of the
machine you describe.

6 The two pictures on pp. 88 and 99 are both detailed and are worth
examining carefully. The photograph of frost on a window-pane
may suggest comparisons to you; pictures may form in your
mind's eye as they do when looking at flames or cloud shapes.
Can you jot down words and phrases to describe the texture of the
frost and the patterns it creates?

In the painting of grasses and plants, Dürer depicts a familiar
sight in great detail. The care with which he does this makes the

The earth from Apollo 8, December 21st, 1968

vegetation seem almost real. Perhaps you could take some every-day subject and make up a word painting.

7 It would be difficult to find two pictures that suggest more dis-similar ways of life than those reproduced on pp. 84–5 and 95. What seems to you to be the predominant mood and atmosphere of each picture? In which sort of background would you rather live and work, and why? What sort of people do you think each environ-ment would be likely to produce? After discussing the pictures you may feel that you can write a piece of your own either related directly to one of them or arising from some aspect of your discussion.

8 On p. 102 we have printed the well-known photograph of the earth as seen from Apollo 8 on 21 December 1968 during its journey towards the moon. Visible is nearly the entire Western Hemisphere, from the mouth of the St. Lawrence River, including nearby New-foundland, to Tierra del Fuego at the southern tip of South America. Central America is clearly outlined. Nearly all of South America is covered by clouds except the high Andes mountain chain along the west coast. A small portion of the bulge of West Africa shows along the sunset terminator.

What are your feelings on seeing the earth reduced to this?

What details strike you most about the picture?

Can you find suitable comparisons to describe the clouds in the area of the sunset?

There are many ideas for a piece of creative writing here.

SATIRES AND OPINIONS

Meditatio

When I carefully consider the curious habits of dogs
I am compelled to conclude
That man is the superior animal.

When I consider the curious habits of man
I confess, my friend, I am puzzled.

EZRA POUND

Satires of Circumstance. II – In Church

'And now to God the Father', he ends,
And his voice thrills up to the topmost tiles:
Each listener chokes as he bows and bends,
And emotion pervades the crowded aisles.
Then the preacher glides to the vestry-door,
And shuts it, and thinks he is seen no more.

The door swings softly ajar meanwhile,
And a pupil of his in the Bible class,
Who adores him as one without gloss or guile,
Sees her idol stand with a satisfied smile
And re-enact at the vestry-glass
Each pulpit gesture in deft dumb-show
That had moved the congregation so.

THOMAS HARDY

VI – In the Cemetery

'You see those mothers squabbling there?'
Remarks the man of the cemetery.
'One says in tears, *"Tis mine lies here!"*
Another, *"Nay, mine, you Pharisee!"*
Another, *"How dare you move my flowers
And put your own on this grave of ours!"*
But all their children were laid therein
At different times, like sprats in a tin.

'And then the main drain had to cross,
And we moved the lot some nights ago,
And packed them away in the general foss
With hundreds more. But their folks don't know,
And as well cry over a new-laid drain
As anything else, to ease your pain!'

THOMAS HARDY

In Westminster Abbey

Let me take this other glove off
    As the vox humana swells,
And the beauteous fields of Eden
    Bask beneath the Abbey bells.
Here, where England's statesmen lie,
Listen to a lady's cry.

Gracious Lord, oh bomb the Germans.
    Spare their women for Thy Sake,
And if that is not too easy
    We will pardon Thy Mistake.
But, Gracious Lord, whate'er shall be,
Don't let anyone bomb me.

Keep our Empire undismembered
  Guide our Forces by Thy Hand,
Gallant blacks from far Jamaica,
  Honduras and Togoland;
Protect them Lord in all their fights,
And, even more, protect the whites.

Think of what our Nation stands for,
  Books from Boots' and country lanes,
Free speech, free passes, class distinction,
  Democracy and proper drains.
Lord, put beneath Thy special care
One-eighty-nine Cadogan Square.

Although dear Lord I am a sinner,
  I have done no major crime;
Now I'll come to Evening Service
  Whensoever I have the time.
So, Lord, reserve for me a crown,
And do not let my shares go down.

I will labour for Thy Kingdom,
  Help our lads to win the war,
, Send white feathers to the cowards
  Join the Women's Army Corps,
Then wash the Steps around Thy Throne
In the Eternal Safety Zone.

Now I feel a little better,
  What a treat to hear Thy Word,
Where the bones of leading statesmen,
  Have so often been interr'd.
And now, dear Lord, I cannot wait
Because I have a luncheon date.

JOHN BETJEMAN

Dooley Is a Traitor

'So then you won't fight?'
'Yes, your Honour,' I said, 'that's right.'
'Now is it that you simply aren't willing,
Or have you a fundamental moral objection to killing?'
Says the judge, blowing his nose
And making his words stand to attention in long rows.
I stand to attention too, but with half a grin
(In my time I've done a good many in).
'No objection at all, sir,' I said.
'There's a deal of the world I'd rather see dead –
Such as Johnny Stubbs or Fred Settle or my last landlord, Mr.
    Syme,
Give me a gun and your blessing, your Honour, and I'll be
    shooting them all the time.
But my conscience says a clear no
To killing a crowd of gentlemen I don't know.
Why, I'd as soon think of killing a worshipful judge,
High-court, like yourself (against whom, God knows, I've got
    no grudge –
So far), as murder a heap of foreign folk.
If you've got no grudge, you've got no joke
To laugh at after.'
                    Now the words never come flowing
Proper for me till I get the old pipe going.
And just as I was poking
Down baccy, the judge looks up sharp with 'No smoking,
Mr. Dooley. We're not fighting this war for fun.
And we want a clearer reason why you refuse to carry a gun.
This war is not a personal feud, it's a fight
Against wrong ideas on behalf of the Right.
Mr. Dooley, won't you help to destroy evil ideas?'
'Ah, your Honour, here's
The tragedy,' I said. 'I'm not a man of the mind.
I couldn't find it in my heart to be unkind

107

To an idea. I wouldn't know one if I saw one. I haven't one of
   my own.
So I'd best be leaving other people's alone.'
'Indeed', he sneers at me, 'this defence is
Curious for someone with convictions in two senses.
A criminal invokes conscience to his aid
To support an individual withdrawal from a communal crusade
Sanctioned by God, led by the Church, against a godless,
   churchless nation!'
I asked his Honour for a translation.
'You talk of conscience,' he said, 'What do you know of the
   Christian creed?'
'Nothing, sir, except what I can read.
That's the most you can hope for from us jail-birds.
I just open the Book here and there and look at the words.
And I find when the Lord himself misliked an evil notion
He turned it into a pig and drove it squealing over a cliff into
   the ocean,
And the loony ran away
And lived to think another day.
There was a clean job done and no blood shed!
Everybody happy and forty wicked thoughts drowned dead.
A neat and Christian murder. None of your mad slaughter
Throwing away the brains with the blood and the baby with
   the bathwater.
Now I look at the war as a sportsman. It's a matter of choosing
The decentest way of losing.
Heads or tails, losers or winners,
We all lose, we're all damned sinners.
And I'd rather be with the poor cold people at the wall that's
   shot
Than the blood guilty devils in the firing-line, in Hell and
   keeping hot.'
'But what right, Dooley, what right,' he cried,
'Have you to say the Lord is on your side?'
'That's a dirty crooked question,' back I roared.

'I said not the Lord was on my side, but I was on the side of
the Lord.'
Then he was up at me and shouting,
But by and by he calms: 'Now we're not doubting
Your sincerity, Dooley, only your arguments,
Which don't make sense.'
('Hullo,' I thought, 'that's the wrong way round.
I may be skylarking a bit, but my brainpan's sound.')
Then biting his nail and sugaring his words sweet:
'Keep your head, Mr. Dooley. Religion is clearly not up your
street.
But let me ask you as a plain patriotic fellow
Whether you'd stand there so smug and yellow
If the foe were attacking your own dear sister.'
'I'd knock their brains out, mister,
On the floor,' I said. 'There,' he says kindly, 'I knew you were
no pacifist.
It's your straight duty as a man to enlist.
The enemy is at the door.' You could have downed
Me with a feather. 'Where?' I gasp, looking round.
'Not this door,' he says angered. 'Don't play the clown.
But they're two thousand miles away planning to do us down.
Why, the news is full of the deeds of those murderers and
rapers.'
'Your Eminence,' I said, 'My father told me never to believe
the papers
But to go by my eyes,
And at two thousand miles the poor things can't tell truth from
lies.'
His fearful spectacles glittered like the moon: 'For the last time
what right
Has a man like you to refuse to fight?'
'More right,' I said, 'than you.
You've never murdered a man, so you don't know what it is I
won't do.
I've done it in good hot blood, so haven't I the right to make
bold

109

To declare that I shan't do it in cold?'
Then the judge rises in a great rage
And writes DOOLEY IS A TRAITOR in black upon a page
And tells me I must die.
'What, me?' says I.
'If you still won't fight.'
'Well, yes, your Honour,' I said, 'that's right.'

JAMES MICHIE

next to of course god america i

'next to of course god america i
love you land of the pilgrims' and so forth oh
say can you see by the dawn's early my
country 'tis of centuries come and go
and are no more what of it we should worry
in every language even deafanddumb
thy sons acclaim your glorious name by gorry
by jingo by gee by gosh by gum
why talk of beauty what could be more beaut-
iful than these heroic happy dead
who rushed like lions to the roaring slaughter
they did not stop to think they died instead
then shall the voice of liberty be mute?'

He spoke. And drank rapidly a glass of water

e. e. cummings

Battered mannequin. Photo: Burt Glinn

Sporus

A portrait of Lord Hervey

Yet let me flap this bug with gilded wings,
This painted child of dirt, that stinks and stings;
Whose buzz the witty and the fair annoys,
Yet wit ne'er tastes, and beauty ne'er enjoys:
So well-bred spaniels civilly delight
In mumbling of the game they dare not bite.
Eternal smiles his emptiness betray,
As shallow streams run dimpling all the way.
Whether in florid impotence he speaks,
And, as the prompter breathes, the puppet squeaks;
Or at the ear of Eve, familiar toad!
Half froth, half venom, spits himself abroad,
In puns, or politics, or tales, or lies,
Or spite, or smut, or rhymes, or blasphemies.
His wit all see-saw, between that and this,
Now high, now low, now master up, now miss,
And he himself one vile antithesis.
Amphibious thing! that acting either part,
The trifling head, or the corrupted heart;
Fop at the toilet, flatterer at the board,
Now trips a lady, and now struts a lord.
Eve's tempter thus the Rabbins have express'd,
A cherub's face, a reptile all the rest.
Beauty that shocks you, parts that none will trust,
Wit that can creep, and pride that licks the dust.

(from *Prologue to the Satires*)

ALEXANDER POPE

Rising Five

'I'm rising five,' he said,
'Not four,' and little coils of hair
Unclicked themselves upon his head.
His spectacles, brimful of eyes to stare
At me and the meadow, reflected cones of light
Above his toffee-buckled cheeks. He'd been alive
Fifty-six months or perhaps a week more:
                              not four,
But rising five.

Around him in the field the cells of spring
Bubbled and doubled; buds unbuttoned; shoot
And stem shook out the creases from their frills,
And every tree was swilled with green.
It was the season after blossoming,
Before the forming of the fruit:
                              not May,
But rising June.

              And in the sky
The dust dissected in the tangential light:
                              not day,
But rising night;
              not now,
But rising soon.

The new buds push the old leaves from the bough.
We drop our youth behind us like a boy
Throwing away his toffee wrappers. We never see the flower,
But only the fruit in the flower; never the fruit,
But only the rot in the fruit. We look for the marriage bed
In the baby's cradle, we look for the grave in the bed:
                              not living,
But rising dead.

NORMAN NICHOLSON

113

A Consumer's Report

The name of the product I tested is LIFE.
I have completed the form you sent me
and understand that my answers are confidential.

I had it as a gift,
I didn't feel much while using it,
in fact, I think I'd have liked to be more excited.
It seemed gentle on the hands
but left an embarrassing deposit behind.
It was not economical
and I have used much more than I thought
(I suppose I have about half left
but it's difficult to tell) –
Although the instructions are fairly large
there are so many of them
I don't know which to follow, especially
as they seem to contradict each other.
I'm not sure such a thing
should be put in the way of children
(heaven knows they're growing up
quickly enough already);
it's difficult to think of a purpose
for it. One of my friends says
it's just to keep its maker in a job.
Also the price is much too high.
Things are piling up so fast,
after all, the world got by
for a thousand million years
without this, do we need it now?
(Incidentally, please ask your man
to stop calling me 'the respondent';
I don't like the sound of it.)
There seem to be a lot of different labels,
sizes and colours should be uniform,
the shape is awkward, it's waterproof

but not heat-resistant, it doesn't keep
yet it's very difficult to get rid of.
Whenever they make it cheaper they seem
to put less in: if you say you don't
want it, then it's delivered anyway –
I'd agree it's a popular product,
it's got into the language; people
even say they're on the side of it.
Personally I think it's overdone,
a small thing people are ready
to behave badly about. I think
we should take it for granted. If its
experts are called philosophers or market
researchers or historians, we shouldn't
care. We are the consumers and the last
law makers. So finally, I'd buy it.
But the question of a 'best buy'
I'd like to leave until I get
the competitive product you said you'd send.

PETER PORTER

Girl Reporter

Fact is her fiction. Sitting in the bar
Raincoat still on, crossed nylon legs revealing
Less than we think, a male in tow and smiling –
Her narrowed eyes flick past to register
Whether I am a story in the offing.

Life is material for her creation.
The doll by the upturned scooter – that is real,
Its head, see, stains the kerb. She runs to call
The news-desk first, then after the police-station,
Already mapping the story of the trial.

115

Errors of fact are part of her prose style.
With every slashing cross-head some truth lies.
In love? She knows. You hate her? She knows. You'll
Cure cancer? reach the moon? Her face may smile –
You're placed by those all-knowing know-all eyes.

What chance has truth against such showy error?
We're butterflies pinned down by this young lady,
Facts of our lives are melted down for cliché.
Even as I write her gaze observes my tremor –
Her lethal pencil always at the ready.

PHILIP HOBSBAUM

The Projectionist's Nightmare

This is the projectionist's nightmare:
A bird finds its way into the cinema,
finds the beam, flies down it,
smashes into a screen depicting a garden,
a sunset and two people being nice to each other.
Real blood, real intestines, slither down
the likeness of a tree.
'This is no good,' screams the audience,
'This is not what we came to see.'

BRIAN PATTEN

When I Went to the Film

When I went to the film, and saw all the black-and-white
    feelings that nobody felt,
and heard the audience sighing and sobbing with all the
    emotions they none of them felt,
and saw them cuddling with rising passions they none of
    them for a moment felt,
and caught them moaning from close-up kisses, black-and-
    white kisses that could not be felt,

116

it was like being in heaven, which I am sure has a white
   atmosphere
upon which shadows of people, pure personalities
are cast in black and white, and move
in flat ecstasy, supremely unfelt,
and heavenly.

D. H. LAWRENCE

Creative Writing

You will already be familiar with the satirical work of political
cartoonists in daily newspapers and probably with satirical pop
songs, and may well know that satire directly ridicules or makes
biting comments on social or political life. The satirist feels indignant
about someone or something: he is the sort of person who protests
not by marching or sitting down or waving banners but by wielding
his pen.

The satirical poet also wishes to change some particular aspect
of a person's behaviour or some injustice in our society, and to
achieve this end he will use all sorts of tricks. Like the political
cartoonist he may exaggerate the physical features of his victim or
dramatise the absurdities of a particular situation. In either case his
aim is to make us laugh at his subject, not simply with the intention
of entertaining us, but, more importantly, to make us think about
why we tolerate such people as Sporus (p. 112) or the hypocritical
clergyman (p. 104). He forces us to question why, despite the defects
implied in the poems on pp. 105 and 107, we continue to value such
institutions as the church and the law.

In writing your own satirical poems you will obviously have to
choose a subject about which you feel particularly strongly, and the
suggestions below can only cover a limited number of topics about
which you *might* feel indignant.

1 The lines about Sporus on p. 112 are in fact a portrait of Lord
   Hervey, an important political figure of his time. Perhaps you
   could write a satirical description of a well-known contemporary
   politician. If political figures do not appeal to you then you may
   be able to satirise someone else in the public eye – a T.V. per-
   sonality, a pop-singer, a film star. (A newspaper photograph in
   front of you will help a lot here.)

117

If you feel confident enough you could try to write in the form used by Pope – rhyming couplets – but there is no reason why you should not write in something less restrictive, such as free verse.

2 We all know people who are proud or conceited about various things, for example, their intelligence, their way of dressing, their way of speaking. Perhaps you could satirise one of these aspects of pride in a poem. You may be able to draw your portrait from life, or imagine a person with one of these characteristics.

3 In Pope's portrait of Sporus (p. 112) and in books like George Orwell's *Animal Farm*, animals and insects are used by the writer to belittle and ridicule his subject. Indeed, in everyday speech we tend to use animal metaphors to attack or criticise people we dislike or whose actions we disapprove of. By calling a person 'a filthy swine' or 'an ass' we suggest he has lost his powers of reason and is simply acting instinctively.

Try to think of a person whom you dislike. Ask yourself how this person resembles a particular creature, both physically and in the way he behaves, and attempt a satirical portrait in verse.

4 In the poem on p. 114 Peter Porter uses the advertising man's Consumer Report to make an ironic comment on the nature of human life. After you have read the poem carefully, you will, of course, realise what 'competitive product' is referred to in the last line. Perhaps you could write your own consumer report on the other product.

5 Philip Hobsbaum's portrait (on p. 115) of the girl reporter shows us rather a hard-bitten character. Try to write a word-portrait of a similar type of person whose job requires him to be warm and sociable on the outside but who may well be just as hard and calculating as the reporter. You might choose to write about a fashion model or a salesman, for example. . . . there are many others.

6 The photographer, like the writer, can put together ideas in such a way as to express his opinions strongly. The photograph on p. 111 comments strikingly on a familiar scene in modern life – an urban riot involving soldiers, tear gas, the destruction of property and so on.

Perhaps you could write about your attitudes and feelings towards mob violence (most of you will have seen examples of this on television). Alternatively, the photograph may suggest other ideas of your own which you could make into a poem.

118

WAR

The Rear-Guard

(*Hindenburg Line, April 1917*)

Groping along the tunnel, step by step,
He winked his prying torch with patching glare
From side to side, and sniffed the unwholesome air.

Tins, boxes, bottles, shapes too vague to know;
A mirror smashed, the mattress from a bed;
And he, exploring fifty feet below
The rosy gloom of battle overhead.

Tripping, he grabbed the wall; saw some one lie
Humped at his feet, half-hidden by a rug,
And stooped to give the sleeper's arm a tug.
'I'm looking for headquarters.' No reply.
'God blast your neck!' (For days he'd had no sleep,)
'Get up and guide me through this stinking place.'

Savage, he kicked a soft, unanswering heap,
And flashed his beam across the livid face
Terribly glaring up, whose eyes yet wore
Agony dying hard ten days before;
And fists of fingers clutched a blackening wound.

Alone he staggered on until he found
Dawn's ghost that filtered down a shafted stair
To the dazed, muttering creatures underground
Who hear the boom of shells in muffled sound.
At last, with sweat of horror in his hair,
He climbed through darkness to the twilight air,
Unloading hell behind him step by step.

SIEGFRIED SASSOON

The Dead-Beat

He dropped, – more sullenly than wearily,
Lay stupid like a cod, heavy like meat,
And none of us could kick him to his feet;
Just blinked at my revolver, blearily;
– Didn't appear to know a war was on,
Or see the blasted trench at which he stared.
'I'll do 'em in,' he whined. 'If this hand's spared,
I'll murder them, I will.'

                A low voice said,
'It's Blighty, p'raps, he sees; his pluck's all gone,
Dreaming of all the valiant, that aren't dead:
Bold uncles, smiling ministerially;
Maybe his brave young wife, getting her fun
In some new home, improved materially.
It's not these stiffs have crazed him; nor the Hun.'

We sent him down at last, out of the way.
Unwounded; – stout lad, too, before that strafe.
Malingering? Stretcher-bearers winked, 'Not half!'

Next day I heard the Doc.'s well-whiskied laugh:
'That scum you sent last night soon died. Hooray.'

                WILFRED OWEN

Asleep

Under his helmet, up against his pack,
After the many days of working and waking,
Sleep took him by the brow and laid him back.
And in the happy no-time of his sleeping,
Death took him by the heart. There was a quaking
Of the aborted life within him leaping . . .
Then chest and sleepy arms once more fell slack.

And soon the slow, stray blood came creeping
From the intrusive lead, like ants on track.
. . . . .
Whether his deeper sleep lie shaded by the shaking
Of great wings, and the thoughts that hung the stars,
High-pillowed on calm pillows of God's making
Above these clouds, these rains, these sleets of lead,
And these winds' scimitars;
— Or whether yet his thin and sodden head
Confuses more and more with the low mould,
His hair being one with the grey grass
And finished fields of autumn that are old . . .
Who knows? Who hopes? Who troubles? Let it pass!
He sleeps. He sleeps less tremulous, less cold,
Than we who must awake, and waking, say Alas!

WILFRED OWEN

Christmas: 1924

'Peace upon earth!' was said. We sing it,
And pay a million priests to bring it.
After two thousand years of mass
We've got as far as poison gas.

THOMAS HARDY

121

First World War recruiting poster. *Imperial War Museum*

The Hero

'Jack fell as he'd have wished,' the Mother said,
And folded up the letter that she'd read.
'The Colonel writes so nicely.' Something broke
In the tired voice that quavered to a choke.
She half looked up. 'We mothers are so proud
Of our dead soldiers.' Then her face was bowed.

Quietly the Brother Officer went out.
He'd told the poor old dear some gallant lies
That she would nourish all her days, no doubt.
For while he coughed and mumbled, her weak eyes
Had shone with gentle triumph, brimmed with joy,
Because he'd been so brave, her glorious boy.

He thought how 'Jack', cold-footed, useless swine,
Had panicked down the trench that night the mine
Went up at Wicked Corner; how he'd tried
To get sent home, and how, at last, he died,
Blown to small bits. And no one seemed to care
Except that lonely woman with white hair.

SIEGFRIED SASSOON

The Soldier

If I should die, think only this of me:
    That there's some corner of a foreign field
That is for ever England. There shall be
    In that rich earth a richer dust concealed;
A dust whom England bore, shaped, made aware,
    Gave, once, her flowers to love, her ways to roam,
A body of England's, breathing English air,
    Washed by the rivers, blest by suns of home.

And think, this heart, all evil shed away,
    A pulse in the eternal mind, no less
        Gives somewhere back the thoughts by England given;
Her sights and sounds; dreams happy as her day;
    And laughter, learnt of friends; and gentleness,
        In hearts at peace, under an English heaven.

RUPERT BROOKE

Dulce et Decorum Est

Bent double, like old beggars under sacks,
Knock-kneed, coughing like hags, we cursed through sludge,
Till on the haunting flares we turned our backs,
And towards our distant rest began to trudge.
Men marched asleep. Many had lost their boots,
But limped on, blood-shod. All went lame, all blind;
Drunk with fatigue; deaf even to the hoots
Of gas-shells dropping softly behind.

Gas! GAS! Quick, boys! — An ecstasy of fumbling,
Fitting the clumsy helmets just in time,
But someone still was yelling out and stumbling
And floundering like a man in fire or lime. —
Dim through the misty panes and thick green light,
As under a green sea, I saw him drowning.

In all my dreams before my helpless sight
He plunges at me, guttering, choking, drowning.

If in some smothering dreams, you too could pace
Behind the wagon that we flung him in,
And watch the white eyes writhing in his face,
His hanging face, like a devil's sick of sin;
If you could hear at every jolt, the blood
Come gargling from the froth-corrupted lungs,
Bitter as the cud
Of vile, incurable sores on innocent tongues, —
My friend, you would not tell with such high zest
To children ardent for some desperate glory,
The old Lie: *Dulce et decorum est*
Pro patria mori.

WILFRED OWEN

First World War recruiting poster. *Imperial War Museum*

All Day It Has Rained

All day it has rained, and we on the edge of the moors
Have sprawled in our bell-tents, moody and dull as boors,
Groundsheets and blankets spread on the muddy ground
And from the first grey wakening we have found
No refuge from the skirmishing fine rain
And the wind that made the canvas heave and flap
And the taut wet guy-ropes ravel out and snap.
All day the rain has glided, wave and mist and dream,
Drenching the gorse and heather, a gossamer stream
Too light to stir the acorns that suddenly
Snatched from their cups by the wild south-westerly
Pattered against the tent and our upturned dreaming faces.
And we stretched out, unbuttoning our braces,
Smoking a Woodbine, darning dirty socks,
Reading the Sunday papers – I saw a fox
And mentioned it in the note I scribbled home; –
And we talked of girls and dropping bombs on Rome,
And thought of the quiet dead and the loud celebrities
Exhorting us to slaughter, and the herded refugees;
– Yet thought softly, morosely of them, and as indifferently
As of ourselves or those whom we
For years have loved, and will again
Tomorrow maybe love; but now it is the rain
Possesses us entirely, the twilight and the rain.

And I can remember nothing dearer or more to my heart
Than the children I watched in the woods on Saturday
Shaking down burning chestnuts for the schoolyard's merry
  play,
Or the shaggy patient dog who followed me
By Sheet and Steep and up the wooded scree
To the Shoulder o' Mutton where Edward Thomas brooded
  long
On death and beauty – till a bullet stopped his song.

ALUN LEWIS

Judging Distances

Not only how far away, but the way that you say it
Is very important. Perhaps you may never get
The knack of judging a distance, but at least you know
How to report on a landscape: the central sector,
The right of arc and that, which we had last Tuesday,
    And at least you know

That maps are of time, not place, so far as the army
Happens to be concerned — the reason being,
Is one which need not delay us. Again, you know
There are three kinds of tree, three only, the fir and the poplar,
And those which have bushy tops to; and lastly
    That things only seem to be things.

A barn is not called a barn, to put it more plainly,
Or a field in the distance, where sheep may be safely grazing.
You must never be over-sure. You must say, when reporting:
At five o'clock in the central sector is a dozen
Of what appear to be animals; whatever you do,
    Don't call the bleeders *sheep.*

I am sure that's quite clear; and suppose, for the sake of
    example,
The one at the end, asleep, endeavours to tell us
What he sees over there to the west, and how far away,
After first having come to attention. There to the west,
On the fields of summer the sun and the shadows bestow
    Vestments of purple and gold.

The still white dwellings are like a mirage in the heat,
And under the swaying elms a man and a woman
Lie gently together. Which is, perhaps, only to say
That there is a row of houses to the left of arc,
And that under some poplars a pair of what appear to be
    humans
    Appear to be loving.

Well that, for an answer, is what we might rightly call
Moderately satisfactory only, the reason being,
Is that two things have been omitted, and those are important.
The human beings, now: in what direction are they,
And how far away, would you say? And do not forget
    There may be dead ground in between.

There may be dead ground in between; and I may not have got
The knack of judging a distance; I will only venture
A guess that perhaps between me and the apparent lovers,
(Who, incidentally, appear by now to have finished),
At seven o' clock from the houses, is roughly a distance
    Of about one year and a half.

HENRY REED

Undivided Loyalty

Nothing is worth dying for.
Some people would rather
Be dead than Red.
But I would simply rather
Not be dead.

I would not die for Britain
Or any land. Why should I?
I only happened to be born there.
Emigré, banished, why should I defend
A land I never chose, that never wanted me?

I might have been born anywhere –
In mid-Pacific or in Ecuador.
I would not die for the world.
Jesus was wrong.
Only nothing is worth dying for.

JAMES KIRKUP

High Wood

Ladies and gentlemen, this is High Wood,
Called by the French, Bois des Fourneaux,
The famous spot which in Nineteen-Sixteen,
July, August and September was the scene
Of long and bitterly contested strife,
By reason of its High commanding site.
Observe the effect of shell-fire in the trees
Standing and fallen; here is wire; this trench
For months inhabited, twelve times changed hands;
(They soon fall in), used later as a grave.
It has been said on good authority
That in the fighting for this patch of wood
Were killed somewhere above eight thousand men,
Of whom the greater part were buried here,
This mound on which you stand being . . .

                                    Madame, please,

You are requested kindly not to touch
Or take away the Company's property
As souvenirs; you'll find we have on sale
A large variety, all guaranteed.
As I was saying, all is as it was,
This is an unknown British officer,
The tunic having lately rotted off.
Please follow me – this way . . .

                        the *path*, sir, *please*,

The ground which was secured at great expense
The Company keeps absolutely untouched,
And in that dug-out (genuine) we provide
Refreshments at a reasonable rate.
You are requested not to leave about
Paper, or ginger-beer bottles, or orange-peel,
There are waste-paper baskets at the gate.

PHILIP JOHNSTONE

Song of the Dying Gunner A.A.1

Oh mother my mouth is full of stars
As cartridges in the tray
My blood is a twin-branched scarlet tree
And it runs all runs away.

Oh *Cooks to the Galley* is sounded off
And the lads are down in the mess
But I lie done by the forrard gun
With a bullet in my breast.

Don't send me a parcel at Christmas time
Of socks and nutty and wine
And don't depend on a long weekend
By the Great Western Railway line.

Farewell, Aggie Weston[1], the Barracks
   at Guz[2],
Hang my tiddley suit on the door
I'm sewn up neat in a canvas sheet
And I shan't be home no more.

CHARLES CAUSLEY

on *H.M.S. Glory*

[1]'Aggie Weston's' is the familiar term used by sailors to describe hostels founded in many seaports by Dame Agnes Weston
[2]'Guz' is Naval slang for Devonport

Survivors

With the ship burning in their eyes
The white faces float like refuse
In the darkness – the water screwing
Oily circles where the hot steel lies.

They clutch with fingers frozen into claws
The lifebelts thrown from a destroyer,
And see, between the future's doors,
The gasping entrance of the sea.

Taken on board as many as lived, who
Had a mind left for living and the ocean,
They open eyes running with surf,
Heavy with the grey ghosts of explosion.

The meaning is not yet clear,
Where daybreak died in the smile –
And the mouth remained stiff
And grinning, stupid for a little while.

But soon they joke, easy and warm,
As men will who have died once
Yet somehow were able to find their way –
Muttering this was not included in their pay.

Later, sleepless at night, the brain spinning
With cracked images, they won't forget
The confusion and the oily dead,
Nor yet the casual knack of living.

ALAN ROSS

The Responsibility

I am the man who gives the word,
If it should come, to use the Bomb.

I am the man who spreads the word
From him to them if it should come.

I am the man who gets the word
From him who spreads the word from him.

I am the man who drops the Bomb
If ordered by the one who's heard
From him who merely spreads the word
The first one gives if it should come.

I am the man who loads the Bomb
That he must drop should orders come
From him who gets the word passed on
By one who waits to hear from *him*.

I am the man who makes the Bomb
That he must load for him to drop
If told by one who gets the word
From one who passes it from *him*.

I am the man who fills the till,
Who pays the tax, who foots the bill
That guarantees the Bomb he makes
For him to load for him to drop
If orders come from one who gets
The word passed on to him by one
Who waits to hear it from the man
Who gives the word to use the Bomb.

I am the man behind it all;
I am the one responsible.

PETER APPLETON

One of Britain's atomic explosions. *Photo: U.K. Atomic Energy Authority*

Creative Writing

In the corresponding section of Book Three we suggested some of the dangers and advantages of trying to write war poems from your own second-hand experience of war. Whether or not you recall this section, it will be helpful to discuss amongst yourselves why you imagine we think this subject may present dangers and difficulties and why, on balance, we decided that this is a worthwhile and valuable experience.

In Book Three we concentrated mainly on poems which described the people and incidents in war, many of them from the 1914–18 period. Here, there are more poems from the Second World War, several of which may provoke you to think more deeply about the rights and wrongs of warfare.

1 Look again at *High Wood* (p. 131), *The Responsibility* (p. 134) and *Undivided Loyalty* (p. 130). After discussing some of the questions that these poems raise, you may be able to summarise your own thoughts on war as a means of nations solving their problems.

2 The two poems on pp. 122 and 123 are about heroism and the ideal of dying for one's country. Read these and talk about them in relation to the two recruiting posters on pp. 122 and 125. You might find an idea for a poem here.

3 Goya's picture on pp. 128–9 shows one of many atrocities perpetrated against Spanish citizens by Napoleon's troops in 1808 after the invasion of Spain. After talking about the details of the picture – the faces of the people, the attitude of the soldiers – you may be able to write about this scene or some other savage aspect of war.

4 Talk to your parents or grandparents about air-raids. Try to build up a picture of what these meant to a family. What was the first indication of a raid? Did the family have a shelter? What was it like to be inside it, waiting and listening? What sounds stick in the memory? What was the neighbourhood like after a raid? If you jot down some notes about these and any other questions that occur to you, you may well find the material for a poem.

5 Read Philip Johnstone's poem *High Wood* (p. 131) carefully. Perhaps you can imagine that you are an old soldier who survived the action at Bois des Fourneaux and who is now listening to the glib patter of the guide. Try to write a poem expressing what your feelings would be about this commercialisation of war.

6 The picture on p. 135 shows what the young protesters on p. 55 are demonstrating against. What are your feelings as you look at this image of power and destruction? (It is perhaps worth noting that this was a relatively small atomic explosion and that present-day weapons are capable of producing an effect many times greater.)

What comparisons come to mind as you look at the shape of the atomic cloud as it hangs in the air and at the base of the pillar where the explosion spreads out over the land?

Try to find phrases and comparisons to describe the shock waves criss-crossing the sky.

The picture may suggest a piece of writing.

SCHOOL

The Play Way

Sunlight pillars through glass, probes each desk
For milk-tops, drinking straws and old dry crusts.
The music strides to challenge it
Mixing memory and desire with chalk dust.

My lesson notes read: Teacher will play
Beethoven's Concerto Number Five
And class will express themselves freely
In writing. One said 'Can we jive?'

When I produced the record, but now
The big sound has silenced them. Higher
And firmer, each authoritative note
Pumps the classroom up tight as a tyre

Working its private spell behind eyes
That stare wide. They have forgotten me
For once. The pens are busy, the tongues mime
Their blundering embrace of the free

Word. A silence charged with sweetness
Breaks short on lost faces where I see
New looks. Then notes stretch taut as snares. They trip
To fall into themselves unknowingly.

SEAMUS HEANEY

138

The Lesson

A tree enters and says with a bow:
    I am a tree.
A black tear falls from the sky and says:
    I am a bird.

Down a spider's web
    something like love
        comes near
            and says:
                I am silence.

But by the blackboard sprawls
    a national democratic
    horse in his waistcoat
    and repeats,
    pricking his ears on every side,
    repeats and repeats
        I am the engine of history
        and
        we all
        love
        progress
        and
        courage
        and
        the fighters' wrath.

Under the classroom door
trickles
a thin stream of blood.

For here begins
the massacre
of the innocents.

                MIROSLAV HOLUB
        (Trans. I. Milner and G. Theiner)

A History Lesson

Kings
like golden gleams
made with a mirror on the wall.

A non-alcoholic pope,
knights without arms,
arms without knights.

The dead like so many strained noodles,
a pound of those fallen in battle,
two ounces of those who were executed,

several heads
like so many potatoes
shaken into a cap —

Geniuses conceived
by the mating of dates
are soaked up by the ceiling into infinity

to the sound of tinny thunder,
the rumble of bellies,
shouts of hurrah,

empires rise and fall
at a wave of the pointer,
the blood is blotted out —

And only one small boy,
who was not paying the least attention,
will ask
between two victorious wars:

And did it hurt in those days too?

MIROSLAV HOLUB
(Trans. I. Milner and G. Theiner)

An Elementary School Class Room in a Slum

Far far from gusty waves these children's faces.
Like rootless weeds, the hair torn round their pallor.
The tall girl with her weighed-down head. The paper-
Seeming boy, with rat's eyes. The stunted, unlucky heir
Of twisted bones, reciting a father's gnarled disease,
His lesson from his desk. At back of the dim class
One unnoted, sweet and young. His eyes live in a dream
Of squirrel's game, in tree room, other than this.

On sour cream walls, donations. Shakespeare's head,
Cloudless at dawn, civilised dome riding all cities.
Belled, flowery, Tyrolese valley. Open-handed map
Awarding the world its world. And yet, for these
Children, these windows, not this world, are world,
Where all their future's painted with a fog,
A narrow street sealed in with a lead sky,
Far far from rivers, capes, and stars of words.

Surely, Shakespeare is wicked, the map a bad example
With ships and sun and love tempting them to steal –
For lives that slyly turn in their cramped holes
From fog to endless night? On their slag heap, these children
Wear skins peeped through by bones and spectacles of steel
With mended glass, like bottle bits on stones.
All of their time and space are foggy slum
So blot their maps with slums as big as doom.

Unless, governor, teacher, inspector, visitor,
This map becomes their window and these windows
Thus shut upon their lives like catacombs,
Break O break open till they break the town
And show the children to green fields, and all their world
Run azure on golden sands, to let their tongues
Run naked into books, the white and green leaves open
History theirs whose language is the sun.

STEPHEN SPENDER

Boys in a Montreal street. *Photo: Henri Cartier-Bresson*

Maladjusted Boys

I have made ten minutes of silence.
I know they are afraid of silence
And the mind's pattern of order.
They gaze at me out of oblique faces
And try to fidget away the bleak thoughts
Simmering in the dark tangle of their minds.
I read their unfriendly eyes, cushion
The confused hatred, stand presumptuously
And pretend not to be afraid.
I keep at them with my eyes,
Will them to work, and ride
The storm in a roomful of cold attention.
Here and there faces cringe
And I read a future . . . the dark corner
Of a street hiding the cruel
Thud of a chain or boot.
I see a hunter mask glow on a face
And grimy nailbitten hands bend a ruler
To its limit . . . all this in a room
Yellow with June sun and music
Of birds from a private wood.

ROBERT MORGAN

144

Thirteen Ways of Looking at a Blackboard

I
The blackboard is clean.
The master must be coming.

II
The vigilant mosquito bites on a rising pitch.
The chalk whistles over the blackboard.

III
Among twenty silent children
The only moving thing
Is the chalk's white finger.

IV
O young white cricketers,
Aching for the greensward,
Do you not see how my moving hand
Whitens the black board?

V
A man and a child
Are one.
And man and a child and a blackboard
Are three.

VI
Some wield their sticks of chalk
Like torches in dark rooms.
I make up my blackboard
Like the face of an actor.

VII
I was of three minds
Like a room
In which there are three blackboards.

VIII
I dream.
I am an albino.

IX
I wake.
I forget a word.
The chalk snaps on the blackboard.

X
Twenty silent children
Staring at the blackboard.
On one wall of each of twenty nurseries
The light has gone out.

XI
He ambles among the white rocks of Dover,
Crushing pebbles with black boots.
He is a small blackboard
Writing on chalk.

XII
It is the Christmas holidays.
The white snow lies in the long black branches.
The black board
In the silent schoolroom
Perches on two stubby branches.

XIII
The flesh that is white
Wastes over the bones that are chalk,
Both in the day
And through the black night.

PETER REDGROVE

Schoolboy

Before playtime let us consider the possibilities
of getting stoned on milk.

    In his dreams,
scribbling overcharged on woodbines,
mumbling obscure sentences into his desk
'No way of getting out,
no way out . . .'
               Poet dying of
too much education, schoolfriends, examinations,
canes that walk the nurseries of his wet dreams;
satchels full of chewing gum, bad jokes, pencils;
crude drawings performed in the name of art. Soon will
come the Joyful Realisation in Mary's back kitchen
        while mother's out.
All this during chemistry.

(The headmaster's crying in his study.
His old pinstripe pants rolled up to his knees
in a vain attempt to recapture youth; emotions
skid along his slippery age; Love, smeared across his face,
like a road accident.)

The schoolyard's full of people to hate.
Full of tick and prefects and a fat schoolmaster
and whistles and older and younger boys, but
he's growing
   sadly
     growing
       up.

Girls,
   becoming mysterious, are now more important
than arriving at school late or receiving trivial awards.
Postcards of those huge women
        seem a little more believable now.

147

(Secretly, the pale, unmarried headmaster telling him
Death is the only grammatically correct full-
                                                    stop.)

Girls,
    still mysterious;
arithmetic thighed, breasts measured in thumbprints,
not inches.
Literature's just another way out.
History's full of absurd mistakes.
King Arthur if he ever existed
would only have farted and excused himself
from the Round Table in a hurry.

(The headmaster, staring through the study window
into the playground, composes evil poems about
the lyrical boy in class four)
                    'He invited us up sir,
                but not for the cane,
                    said the algebra of life
                        was too difficult to explain
                        and that all equations
                            mounted to nothing. . . .'

Growing up's wonderful if
                you keep your eyes
                    closed tightly, and
if you manage to grow
            take your soul with you,
                nobody wants it.

So,
playtime's finished with;
it's time to pull the last sad chain
            on his last
            sadschoolgirlcrush.

It is time to fathom out too many things.
To learn he's no longer got somebody watching over him;
he's going to know strange things, learn
how to lie correctly, how to lay correctly,
how to cheat and steal in the nicest possible manner.
He will learn amongst other things, how to enjoy
his enemies, and how to avoid friendships. If he's unlucky
he will learn how to love and give everything away
and how eventually, he'll end up with nothing.

      He won't understand many things.
He'll just accept them. He'll experiment with hardboiled
      eggs all his life
and die a stranger in a race attempting Humanity.

    And finally,
the playground full of dust,
      crates of sour milk lining the corridors;
        the headmaster, weeping quietly among the saws and
                            chisels
      in the damp woodwork room;

      The ghosts of Tim and Maureen and Pat
       and Nancy and so many others,
   all holding sexless hands, all
        doomed to living, and
one pale boy
in a steamy room
looking outside across the roofs and chimneys
where it seems, the clouds are crying,
the daylight's gone blind
and his teachers, all dead.

BRIAN PATTEN

Creative Writing

1 Many adults, when they revisit a school long after they themselves have left, find that the atmosphere of school suddenly floods back to their memories. Certain sounds — the noise of the playground, the clatter of feet down corridors, bells; certain smells — chalk dust, wet raincoats in the cloakroom, science laboratories; certain sights — the school clock, row of desks, the dining-hall — all of these immediately remind them of what it was like to be at school. It is true that certain areas of any school have an atmosphere of their own. Perhaps you could write about one of these, for example, the stock room, cloakroom, gym, assembly hall, workshops, laboratories, library.

2 Are you in a gang or group — perhaps a Youth Club?

Are your leader or led?

What are your feelings towards others in the group and to those outside it?

Why do teenagers have gangs? What do you think of them?

After discussing some of these questions you may find a subject or idea for a piece of writing. The picture on pp. 142 and 143 may help both in your discussion and writing.

3 Read once more *Thirteen Ways of Looking at a Blackboard* on p. 145. This way of looking at things could be applied to any number of objects, but try it first with other familiar pieces of classroom equipment: a piece of chalk, a ruler, your desk — there are many possibilities here for some writing modelled on Peter Redgrove's poem.

4 Some of you will have been punished for a misdemeanour in school perhaps by being put in detention or having to see the head teacher. Try to think about a specific occasion of this sort, and remember your feelings towards the person giving you the punishment and your feelings when receiving it or waiting to receive it.

5 Do you accept your teachers' authority?

Do you help or hinder, generally?

Do you work or waste time, if not pushed?

Look again at R. Morgan's poem *Maladjusted Boys* on p. 144. We are not suggesting that you are maladjusted, but, nevertheless, there may well be some attitudes here with which you sympathise.

In discussing these questions and the poem, you may find an

idea for a piece of writing about your own attitudes towards school.

6 You may have taken part in a school play or read before an audience in assembly. Both these can be very taxing experiences, particularly when first you attempt them. Perhaps you could jot down some ideas of how it feels just before you take the stage, how it affects your voice and manner, how the audience appears to you. For those of you who are often involved in plays perhaps you could make some notes about the excitement of being behind the scenes – the battery of lights, last-minute adjustments to costumes, the smell of greasepaint, nervous laughter. From one of these sets of notes you may be able to write a poem capturing the atmosphere of the occasion.

CREATURES

Esther's Tomcat

Daylong this tomcat lies stretched flat
As an old rough mat, no mouth and no eyes.
Continual wars and wives are what
Have tattered his ears and battered his head.

Like a bundle of old rope and iron
Sleeps till blue dusk. Then reappear
His eyes, green as ringstones: he yawns wide red,
Fangs fine as a lady's needle and bright.

A tomcat sprang at a mounted knight,
Locked round his neck like a trap of hooks
While the knight rode fighting its clawing and bite.
After hundreds of years the stain's there

On the stone where he fell, dead of the tom:
That was at Barnborough. The tomcat still
Grallochs[1] odd dogs on the quiet,   [1]disembowels
Will take the head clean off your simple pullet,

Is unkillable. From the dog's fury,
From gunshot fired point-blank he brings
His skin whole, and whole
From owlish moons of bekittenings

Among ashcans. He leaps and lightly
Walks upon sleep, his mind on the moon
Nightly over the round world of men,
Over the roofs go his eyes and outcry.

TED HUGHES

Old lady with a cat. Photo: Neville Cooper

Cheetah

Indolent and kitten-eyed,
This is the bushveld's innocent –
The stealthy leopard parodied
With grinning, gangling pup-content.

Slouching through the tawny grass
Or loose-limbed lolling in the shade,
Purring for the sun to pass
And build a twilight barricade

Around the vast arena where,
In scattered herds, his grazing prey
Do not suspect in what wild fear
They'll join with him in fatal play;

Till hunger draws slack sinews tight
And vibrant as a hunter's bow:
Then, like a fleck of mottled light,
He slides across the still plateau.

A tremor rakes the herds: they scent
The pungent breeze of his advance;
Heads rear and jerk in vigilant
Compliance with the game of chance

In which, of thousands, only one
Is centred in the cheetah's eye;
They wheel and then stampede, for none
Knows which it is that has to die.

His stealth and swiftness fling a noose
And as his loping strides begin
To blur with speed, he ropes the loose
Buck on the red horizon in.

CHARLES EGLINGTON

Hawk Roosting

I sit in the top of the wood, my eyes closed.
Inaction, no falsifying dream
Between my hooked head and hooked feet:
Or in sleep rehearse perfect kills and eat.

The convenience of the high trees!
The air's buoyancy and the sun's ray
Are of advantage to me;
And the earth's face upward for my inspection.

My feet are locked upon the rough bark.
It took the whole of Creation
To produce my foot, my each feather:
Now I hold Creation in my foot

Or fly up, and revolve it all slowly –
I kill where I please because it is all mine.
There is no sophistry in my body:
My manners are tearing off heads –

The allotment of death.
For the one path of my flight is direct
Through the bones of the living.
No arguments assert my right:

The sun is behind me.
Nothing has changed since I began.
My eye has permitted no change.
I am going to keep things like this.

TED HUGHES

The Maldive Shark

About the Shark, phlegmatical one,
Pale sot of the Maldive sea,
The sleek little pilot fish, azure and slim
How alert in attendance be.
From his saw-pit of mouth, from his charnel of maw
They have nothing of harm to dread,
But liquidly glide on his ghastly flank
Or before his Gorgonian head;
Or lurk in the port of serrated teeth
In white triple tiers of glittering gates,
And there find a haven when peril's abroad,
An asylum in jaws of the fates!
They are friends; and friendly they guide him to prey,
Yet never partake of the treat –
Eyes and brains to the dotard lethargic and dull,
Pale ravener of horrible meat.

HERMAN MELVILLE

Leviathan

A puff-adder, khaki,
fatter than a stocking of pus
except for its short thin tail,
obese and quick
as certain light-footed dancers
took a dozing lizard.

Scaly little monster
with delicate hands and feet
stupidly sluggish in the sun.
Panting, true,
but lizards breathe mostly
as if their lives depended.

Gone.
Enveloped by a slack
wormy yellow bowel.

O Jonah, to tumble to
those sickly deadly depths,
slick walled, implacably black.
DOUGLAS LIVINGSTONE

The Wasps' Nest

All day to the loose tile behind the parapet
The droning bombers fled: in the wet gutter
Belly-upwards the dead were lying, numbed
By October cold. And now the bloat queen,
Sick-orange, with wings draped, and feelers trailing,
Like Helen combing her hair, posed on the ledge
Twenty feet above the traffic. I watched, just a foot
From her eyes, very glad of the hard glass parting
My pressed human nose from her angry sting

And her heavy power to warm the cold future
Sunk in unfertilised eggs. And I thought: if I reached
And inched this window open, and cut her in half
With my unclasped pen-knife, I could exterminate
An unborn generation. All next summer,
If she survives, the stepped roof will swarm
With a jam of striped fighters. Therefore, this winter
In burning sulphur in their dug-out hangars
All the bred wasps must die. Unless I kill her.
So I balanced assassination with genocide
As the queen walked on the ledge, a foot from my eyes
In the last sun of the year, the responsible man
With a cold nose, who knew that he must kill,
Coming to no sure conclusion, nor anxious to come.

GEORGE MacBETH

Frogs

Frogs sit more solid
Than anything sits. In mid-leap they are
Parachutists falling
In a free fall. They die on roads
With arms across their chests and
Heads high.

I love frogs that sit
Like Buddha, that fall without
Parachutes, that die
Like Italian tenors.

Above all, I love them because,
Pursued in water, they never
Panic so much that they fail
To make stylish triangles
With their ballet dancer's
Legs.

NORMAN MacCAIG

Elephants

Tonnage of instinctive
Wisdom in tinsel,
Trunks like questions
And legs like tree trunks

On each forehead
A buxom blonde
And round each leg
A jangle of bells,

Deep in each brain
A chart of tropic
Swamp and twilight
Of creepered curtains,

Shamble in shoddy
Finery forward
And make their salaams
To the tiers of people –

Dummies with a reflex
Muscle of laughter
When they see the mountains
Come to Mahomet. . . .

Efficacy of engines,
Obstinacy of darkness.

LOUIS MacNEICE

The Fox

It was twenty years ago I saw the fox
Gliding along the edge of prickling corn,
A nefarious shadow
Between the emerald field and bristling hedge,
On velvet feet he went.

The wind was kind, withheld from him my scent
Till my threaded gaze unmasked him standing there,
The colour of last year's beech-leaves, pointed black,
Poised, uncertain, quivering nose aware
Of danger throbbing through each licking leaf.
One foot uplifted, balanced on the brink
Of perennial fear, the hunter hunted stood.

I heard no alien stir in the friendly wood,
But the fox's sculpted attitude was tense
With scenting, listening, with a seventh sense
Flaring to the alert; I heard no sound
Threaten the morning; and followed his amber stare,
But in that hair-breadth moment, that flick of the eye,
He vanished.

And now, whenever I hear the expectant cry
Of hounds on the empty air,
I look to ʌ gap in the hedge and see him there
Filling the space with fear; the trembling leaves
Are frozen in his stillness till I hear
His leashed-up breathing − how the stretch of time
Contracts within the flash of re-creation!

PHOEBE HESKETH

Young Hare, *Dürer*

Kangaroo

In the northern hemisphere
Life seems to leap at the air, or skim under the wind
Like stags on rocky ground, or pawing horses, or springy
    scut-tailed rabbits.

Or else rush horizontal to charge at the sky's horizon,
Like bulls or bisons or wild pigs.

Or slip like water slippery towards its ends,
As foxes, stoats, and wolves, and prairie dogs.

Only mice, and moles, and rats, and badgers, and beavers,
    and perhaps bears
Seem belly-plumbed to the earth's mid-navel.
Or frogs that when they leap come flop, and flop to the
    centre of the earth.

But the yellow antipodal Kangaroo, when she sits up,
Who can unseat her, like a liquid drop that is heavy, and
    just touches earth.

The downward drip
The down-urge.
So much denser than cold-blooded frogs.

Delicate mother Kangaroo
Sitting up there rabbit-wise, but huge, plumb-weighted,
And lifting her beautiful slender face, oh! so much more
    gently and finely lined than a rabbit's, or than a hare's,
Lifting her face to nibble at a round white peppermint
    drop which she loves, sensitive mother Kangaroo.

Her sensitive, long, pure-bred face.
Her full antipodal eyes, so dark,
So big and quiet and remote, having watched so many
    empty dawns in silent Australia.

Her little loose hands, and drooping Victorian shoulders.
And then her great weight below the waist, her vast pale
    belly
With a thin young yellow little paw hanging out, and
    straggle of a long thin ear, like ribbon,
Like a funny trimming to the middle of her belly, thin
    little dangle of an immature paw, and one thin ear.

Her belly, her big haunches
And, in addition, the great muscular python-stretch of her
    tail.

There, she shan't have any more peppermint drops.
So she wistfully, sensitively sniffs the air, and then turns,
    goes off in slow sad leaps

On the long flat skis of her legs,
Steered and propelled by that steel-strong snake of a tail.

Stops again, half turns, inquisitive to look back.
While something stirs quickly in her belly, and a lean
    little face comes out, as from a window,

Peaked and a bit dismayed,
Only to disappear again quickly away from the sight of
    the world, to snuggle down in the warmth,
Leaving the trail of a different paw hanging out.

Still she watches with eternal, cocked wistfulness!
How full her eyes are, like the full, fathomless, shining eyes
    of an Australian black-boy
Who has been lost so many centuries on the margins of
    existence!

She watches with insatiable wistfulness.
Untold centuries of watching for something to come,
For a new signal from life, in that silent lost land of the
    South.

Where nothing bites but insects and snakes and the sun,
  small life.
Where no bull roared, no cow ever lowed, no stag cried,
  no leopard screeched, no lion coughed, no dog barked,
But all was silent save for parrots occasionally, in the
  haunted blue bush.

Wistfully watching, with wonderful liquid eyes.
And all her weight, all her blood, dripping sack-wise down
  towards the earth's centre,
And the live little-one taking in its paw at the door of her
  belly.

Leap then, and come down on the line that draws to the
  earth's deep, heavy centre.

                                        D. H. LAWRENCE

Dawn Shoot

Clouds ran their wet mortar, plastered the daybreak
Grey. The stones clicked tartly
If we missed the sleepers but mostly
Silent we headed up the railway
Where now the only steam was funnelling from cows
Ditched on their rumps beyond hedges,
Cudding, watching, and knowing.
The rails scored a bull's-eye into the eye
Of a bridge. A corncrake challenged
Unexpectedly like a hoarse sentry
And a snipe rocketed away on reconnaissance.
Rubber-booted, belted, tense as two parachutists,
We climbed the iron gate and dropped
Into the meadow's six acres of broom, gorse and dew.

A sandy bank, reinforced with coiling roots,
Faced you, two hundred yards from the track.
Snug on our bellies behind a rise of dead whins,
Our ravenous eyes getting used to the greyness,
We settled, soon had the holes under cover.
This was the den they all would be heading for now,
Loping under ferns in dry drains, flashing
Brown orbits across ploughlands and grazing.

The plaster thinned at the skyline, the whitewash
Was bleaching on houses and stables,
The cock would be sounding reveille
In seconds.
And there was one breaking
In from the gap in the corner.

Donnelly's left hand came up
And came down on my barrel. This one was his.
'For Christ's sake,' I spat, 'Take your time, there'll be more.'
There was the playboy trotting up to the hole
By the ash tree, 'Wild rover no more,'
Said Donnelly and emptied two barrels
And got him. I finished him off.

Another snipe catapulted into the light,
A mare whinnied and shivered her haunches
Up on a hill. The others would not be back
After three shots like that. We dandered off
To the railway; the prices were small at that time
So we did not bother to cut out the tongue.
The ones that slipped back when the all clear got round
Would be first to examine him.

SEAMUS HEANEY

... and finished off his bull with a clean stroke of the sword into its brain.

Photo: Daily Express

First Blood

It was. The breech smelling of oil,
The stock of resin – buried snug
In the shoulder. Not too much recoil
At the firing of the first slug

(Jubilantly into the air)
Not yet too little. Targets pinned
Against a tree: shot down: and there
Abandoned to the sniping wind.

My turn first to carry the gun.
Indian file and camouflaged
With contours of green shade and sun
We ghosted between larch and larch.

A movement between branches – thump
Of a fallen cone. The barrel
Jumps, making branches jump
Higher, dislodging the squirrel

To the next tree. Your turn, my turn.
The silhouette retracts its head.
A hit. 'Let's go back to the lawn.'
'We can't leave it carrying lead

For the rest of its life. Reload.
Finish him off. Reload again.'
It was now *him*, and when he showed
The sky cracked like a window pane.

He broke away: traversed a full
Half dozen trees: vanished. Had found
A hole? We watched that terrible
Slow spiral to the clubbing ground.

His back was to the tree. His eyes
Were gun barrels. He was dumb,
And we could not see past the size
Of his hands or hear for the drum

In his side. Four shots point-blank
To dull his eyes, a fifth to stop
The shiver in his clotted flank.
A fling of earth. As we stood up

The larches closed their ranks. And when
Earth would not muffle the drumming blood
We, like dishonoured soldiers, ran
The gauntlet of a darkening wood.

JON STALLWORTHY

Lizard

A lizard ran out on a rock and looked up, listening
no doubt to the sounding of the spheres.
And what a dandy fellow! the right toss of a chin for you
and swirl of a tail!

If men were as much men as lizards are lizards
they'd be worth looking at.

D. H. LAWRENCE

Turkeys Observed

One observes them, one expects them;
Blue-breasted in their indifferent mortuary,
Beached bare on the cold marble slabs
In immodest underwear frills of feather.

The red sides of beef retain
Some of the smelly majesty of living:
A half-cow slung from a hook maintains
That blood and flesh are not ignored.

But a turkey cowers in death.
Pull his neck, pluck him, and look –
He is just another poor forked thing,
A skin bag plumped with inky putty.

He once complained extravagantly
In an overture of gobbles;
He lorded it on the claw-flecked mud
With a grey flick of his Confucian eye.

Now, as I pass the bleak Christmas dazzle,
I find him ranged with his cold squadrons:
The fuselage is bare, the proud wings snapped,
The tail-fan stripped down to a shameful rudder.

SEAMUS HEANEY

Town Owl

On eves of cold, when slow coal fires,
rooted in basements, burn and branch,
brushing with smoke the city air;

When quartered moons pale in the sky,
and neons glow along the dark
like deadly nightshade on a briar;

Above the muffled traffic then
I hear the owl, and at his note
I shudder in my private chair.

For like an augur he has come
to roost among our crumbling walls,
his blooded talons sheathed in fur.

Some secret lure of time it seems
has called him from his country wastes
to hunt a newer wasteland here.

And where the candelabra swung
bright with the dancers' thousand eyes,
now his black, hooded pupils stare,

And where the silk-shoed lovers ran
with dust of diamonds in their hair,
he opens now his silent wing,

And, like a stroke of doom, drops down,
and swoops across the empty hall,
and plucks a quick mouse off the stair. . . .

                         LAURIE LEE

Creative Writing

1 Look at the picture of the old lady and her cat on p. 153. Why is it that people keep pets? What do you think the old lady feels about her cat and its kitten? Perhaps you could write a poem either about her or about the feelings of someone you know who has a pet.

2 Some of you will have dogs as pets and are probably responsible for exercising them. Sometimes you may take the dog for a walk late at night down empty streets. Perhaps you can write a poem which creates the atmosphere and suggests the relationship between you and your dog on such an occasion.

   At other times of the day you might let your dog run free in a public park or wood. Try to write about one of these times.

3 Imagine that you are fishing and that a fish takes the bait. Describe, in a poem, what you see and what you feel from the moment the float dips, through reeling it in and unhooking your catch. Do you kill it? Put it in your keep net? Or throw it back? What does it feel like to handle? What are your feelings as you decide its fate?

4 In the picture of *The Young Hare* on p. 161, notice how Dürer has paid great attention to the tiniest details. Try to create a word-picture in similar detail suggested either by the picture or by one of the following: a hedgehog, a tortoise, a budgerigar in a cage, a goldfish in a bowl, a squirrel, a blackbird tugging at a worm, a rook or a crow, a collection of birds' eggs or butterflies.

5 The poems on pp. 165 and 168 describe two bloodsports. Perhaps it would be useful to discuss in what circumstances killing of animals might be justified. Can you justify killing animals for pleasure?

   It might be relevant to think about trapping animals, stalking and shooting deer, stag hunting, fox hunting, bull fighting, 'the glorious twelfth'. Perhaps you could make a poem which not only describes a bloodsport taking place but also expresses your feelings about it. The picture on pp. 166–7 may help.

6 Louis MacNeice's poem *Elephants* on p. 159 may remind you of a time when you have actually been to a circus or when you have watched one on T.V. If you can recall one of the acts clearly, try to write about it.

   What are your reactions to circus acts involving performing animals? Amusement? Boredom? Distaste? Try not only to describe what you imagine in your mind's eye, but also to record your feelings.

Index of First Lines

173

175

Index of Authors

Sources and Acknowledgements

Thanks are due to the authors (or their executors), their representatives and publishers mentioned in the following list for their kind permission to reproduce copyright material:

Peter Appleton: 'The Responsibility' by permission of the author.

John Betjeman: 'Death in Leamington' and 'In Westminster Abbey' from *Collected Poems*, John Murray (Publishers) Ltd.

Edwin Brock: 'On Being Chosen for a Schools Anthology' from *With Love from Judith*, Scorpion Press.

Charles Causley: 'Song of the Dying Gunner A.A.1' from *Union Street*, Rupert Hart-Davis Ltd., by permission of the author.

Tony Connor: 'Elegy for Alfred Hubbard' and 'Mrs. Root' from *With Love Somehow*, Oxford University Press.

e. e. cummings: 'next to of course god america i' from *Complete Poems 1913–1935*, McGibbon and Kee Ltd.

Emily Dickinson: 'I Felt a Funeral in my Brain' reprinted by permission of the publishers and the trustees of Amherst College from Thomas H. Johnson, Editor, *The Poems of Emily Dickinson*, Cambridge, Mass.: The Belknap Press of Harvard University Press, copyright 1951, 1955 by the President and Fellows of Harvard College.

Keith Douglas: 'Behaviour of Fish in an Egyptian Tea Garden' from *Collected Poems*, Faber and Faber Ltd.

Charles Eglington: 'Cheetah' from *The Oxford Book of South African Verse*, Oxford University Press, by permission of the author.

Lawrence Ferlinghetti: 'Christ Climbed Down' and 'Constantly Risking Absurdity' from *A Coney Island of the Mind*, New Directions Publishing Corporation, by permission of the author.

Robert Frost: 'Forgive O Lord' from *The Poetry of Robert Frost* edited by Edward Connery Latham, Jonathan Cape Ltd., by permission of the estate of Robert Frost.

Robert Graves: 'A Civil Servant' from *Collected Poems 1959*, Cassell and Co. Ltd., by permission of the author.

Michael Hamburger: 'After Christmas' from *The Dual Site*, Routledge and Kegan Paul Ltd., by permission of the author.

Thomas Hardy: 'Afterwards', 'Christmas 1924', 'In the Cemetery', 'Stories of Circumstance in Church' and 'Voices from Things Growing in a Churchyard' from *Collected Poems*, Macmillan and Co. Ltd. and by permission of the estate of Thomas Hardy.

Seamus Heaney: 'Dawn Shoot', 'Digging', 'Docker', 'Follower', 'The Play Way', 'Storm on the Island', 'Turkeys Observed' and 'Waterfall' from *Death of a Naturalist*; 'The Forge' from *Door into the Dark*, Faber and Faber Ltd.

Phoebe Hesketh: 'Prayer for the Sun' from *The Fox*, Rupert Hart-Davis

177

Ezra Pound: 'The Garden' and 'Meditatio' from *Collected Shorter Poems*, Faber and Faber Ltd.

Peter Redgrove: 'Thirteen Ways of Looking at a Blackboard' from *The Collector and Other Poems*, Routledge and Kegan Paul Ltd.

Henry Reed: 'Judging Distances' from *A Map of Verona*, Jonathan Cape Ltd., by permission of the author.

W. R. Rodgers: 'Stormy Day' from *Awake and Other Poems*, Martin Secker and Warburg Ltd.

Theodore Roethke: 'Orchids' from *Collected Poems*, Faber and Faber Ltd.

Alan Ross: 'Survivors' from *Something of the Sea*, Derek Verschoyle.

Siegfried Sassoon: 'The Hero' and 'The Rear-Guard' from *Collected Poems*, Faber and Faber Ltd., by permission of Mr. George Sassoon.

Vernon Scannell: 'After the Fireworks' from *Walking Wounded*, Eyre and Spottiswoode Ltd., by permission of the author.

Stephen Spender: 'An Elementary School Classroom in a Slum' and 'The Pylons' from *Collected Poems 1928-1953*, Faber and Faber Ltd.

Jon Stallworthy: 'First Blood' from *Out of Bounds*, Oxford University Press.

R. S. Thomas: 'The Maker', 'An Old Man', 'Poetry for Supper' and 'Soil' from *Poetry for Supper*, Rupert Hart-Davis Ltd.

Charles Tomlinson: 'The Crane' from *Seeing Is Believing*, Oxford University Press.

Louis Untermeyer: 'Portrait of a Machine', copyright 1923 Harcourt Brace Jovanovitch, Inc., copyright 1951 Louis Untermeyer, reprinted from *Long Feud: Selected Poems* by permission of Harcourt Brace Jovanovitch, Inc.

John Updike: 'Bendix' and 'Telephone Poles' from *Telephone Poles and Other Poems*, André Deutsch.

Arthur Waley: 'The Little Cart' from *170 Chinese Poems*, Constable and Co. Ltd.

Humbert Wolfe: 'The Grey Squirrel' by permission of Ann Wolfe.

The authors wish to thank the following for permission to reproduce photographs:

The Albertina Museum, Vienna: 'The Large Piece of Turf' and 'The Young Hare', Dürer.

Birmingham City Museum and Art Gallery and *The Royal Academy of Arts:* 'February Fill-Dyke', B. W. Leader, R.A.

Bill Brandt: 'Wet roofs'.

Neville Cooper: 'Old lady with a cat'.

Mme Sonia Delaunay and *Sotheby and Co.:* 'The Runners', R. Delaunay.

The John Hillelson Agency Ltd.: 'Battered mannequin', 'Boys in a Montreal street' and 'Shadows, Rome'.

Imperial War Museum: First World War recruiting posters.

Philip Jones Griffiths: 'Protest march'.

London Express News and Feature Service: '. . . and finished off his bull with a clean stroke of the sword into its brain'.

The Museum of Modern Art, New York: 'Landscape: the Persistence of Memory', Salvador Dali.

National Aeronautics and Space Administration, Houston, Texas: 'The earth from Apollo 8, December 21st, 1968'.

C. O'Gorman: 'Frost on a window'.

Mr. Harold Owen, Chatto and Windus Ltd, and *The British Museum:* First draft and Fourth and final draft of 'Anthem for Doomed Youth' by Wilfred Owen.

The Prado Museum, Madrid: 'Shootings of May 3rd, 1808', Goya.

Eric Schneider: 'Man with an advertising board'.

The Trustees of Kupferstichkabin, Berlin, and *Mr. Walter Steinkopf:* 'Portrait of his Mother', Dürer.

U.K. Atomic Energy Authority: 'One of Britain's atomic explosions'.

J. B. Urvater Collection, Brussels: 'The Healer', Magritte.

We wish to thank our mother and our wives for the very considerable help they have given in the preparation of the typescript.

M. G. B.
P. B.

ISBN 0 340 05233 3

First published 1971, reprinted 1973, 1975, 1976

Printed in Great Britain
for Hodder and Stoughton Educational,
a division of Hodder and Stoughton Ltd, London, by
Butler & Tanner Ltd, Frome and London